W9-BEI-303

Chess Choice Challenge 3

Chris Ward

B.T. Batsford Ltd, *London*

First published in 2004
© Chris Ward 2004

ISBN 0 7134 8866 2

British Library Cataloguing-in-Publication Data.
A catalogue record for this book is
available from the British Library.

All rights reserved. No part of this book may be
reproduced, by any means, without prior permission
of the publisher.

Printed in Great Britain by
Creative Print and Design (Wales), Ebbw Vale
for the publishers,
B.T. Batsford Ltd,
The Chrysalis Building
Bramley Road,
London, W10 6SP

Distributed in the United States and Canada by Sterling Publishing Co.,
387 Park Avenue South, New York, NY 10016, USA

D: always!

A BATSFORD CHESS BOOK

Preface

So you're back, from outer space...

Well perhaps not, but I grabbed your attention didn't I? Now I know my memory seems to be fading fast these days but when I compiled these questions I didn't think that in general they were that difficult. Sitting here now though in possession of the proofs, I tell you I'm having trouble solving some of them myself! Indeed reading the answers I'm even learning a thing or two! Although I'm not sure I can bear much of my own sense of humour, presumably that means it can't be too bad!?

Modestly I'd have to say that I quite liked *CCC1* whilst *CCC2* even seemed to pick up reasonable reviews. I can only hope that *CCC3* lives up to the expectations of you, the reader. Thanks for coming back for more.

Chris Ward

Beckenham, November 20th 2003

Contents

"SCORECHART"

Introduction

Are you after wickedly useful theoretical endgames wrapped up in the guise of sensational entertainment?

Are you interested in seeing tactics galore frequently based on recent games?

If your answer to these questions is "Yes" then you have come to the right place (at least I hope so!). Indeed *Chess Choice Challenge 3* provides another bunch of amazingly instructive puzzles(!?) that test your positional understanding as well as your ability to analyse ahead well into the future!

The problem with most chess quizzes is that they are unrealistic. The fact is when you are playing a real game there is no devil or angel that appears to tell you that you have a forced win. With this multiple choice format I have tried to eliminate that element as I provide some reasonable options to encompass a wide range of thought processes. Okay admittedly there is often one blatantly duff answer but be warned, you can't always write off an option purely based on my wording!

Regular readers of these books will know the drill by now. There are twenty questions in each test and each question has a correct answer worth 5 points. Occasionally I may award a point or so for something other than what I have deemed to be the best answer but generally speaking I'm not too generous! Tot up your points at the end and compare your results with those of a friend or rival. Which of you really has the greater understanding of the game? Alternatively if you have no friends, refer to the 100% accurate(?!) performance chart at the back to see just where you appear in the grand scheme of things!

I guess that if *CCC1* had an emphasis on endings and *CCC2* focused more on middlegames, then this text is a kind of mixture of the two! I could say "Don't move the pieces" if you set the positions up on a board when doing these puzzles, but obviously I won't actually know if you are cheating or not! Be sure to read my explanations in the answers at the back though because if you learn something and are entertained then I have done my job.

Well it's time for me to stop yapping. I won't say good luck because this is all about skill. Thanks though for taking this journey and I'll maybe see you again some time (*CCC4?*)!

What is the correct assessment of the position below in which it is White to move?

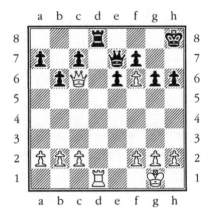

A   Black has the initiative but with best play the game should be a draw.

B   White is slightly better but still the outcome should be a draw.

C   White is actually in quite a lot of trouble. He will lose a pawn by force and in theory the game too.

D   White is winning.

E   'Equal' is a very fair assessment.

A ☐   **B** ☐   **C** ☐   **D** ☐   **E** ☐   **Points**...........

It is White to move below. What is the truth about this and similar queen vs pawn scenarios?

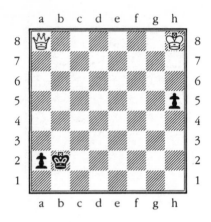

A   Black is lost with or without the presence of the h-pawn.

B   Black holds the draw with or without the h-pawn.

C   Black is lost here but would draw if the h-pawn wasn't in existence.

D   Black is lost here but would draw if the a-pawn wasn't in existence.

E   Black is winning!

A ☐ **B** ☐ **C** ☐ **D** ☐ **E** ☐ **Points**...........

Which statement holds the most truth about this position in which it is White to play?

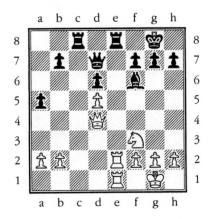

A   Black has the slightly better chances due to his bishop for knight advantage.

B   White has the slightly better chances due to his knight for bishop advantage.

C   Taking everything into consideration things are fairly even.

D   Black isn't exactly winning but he has a clear advantage.

E   White is exactly winning and pretty much by force!

A ☐   **B** ☐   **C** ☐   **D** ☐   **E** ☐   **Points**............

You enter a tournament hall and observe the following position with Black to play still in progress. What can you conclude?

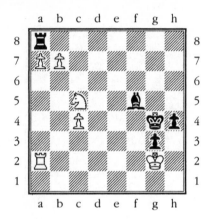

A   The position is illegal!

B   Black will have nothing but a spite check or two. White is winning.

C   Black can force a draw and in this situation that's a good result!

D   Black is in fact winning.

E   It's all very murky!

A ☐ B ☐ C ☐ D ☐ E ☐ **Points**............

Which move most appeals to you for White in the position below?

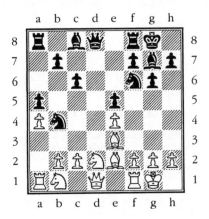

A   Completion of development must be the order of the day. Hence 1 ♘c3.

B   1 ♘a3 develops the knight and retains the option of a c2-c3.

C   White should develop the rook as it is too early to commit the queen's knight. Hence 1 ♖e1.

D   The rook should enter the action via a pawn break. 1 f4 seeks to open the f-file.

E   White should start probing the Black defensive shield with 1 h4 (intending 2 h5) simply jumping out as an obvious plan.

A ☐ **B** ☐ **C** ☐ **D** ☐ **E** ☐ **Points**...........

Yep it's time to get that grey matter working. No moving the pieces as you uncover the truth for Black to play in the simple looking end-game below.

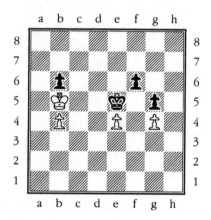

A   Black should obtain the opposition via 1...♔d6.

B   1...♔xe4 would draw but 1...♔f4 would win.

C   1...♔xe4 would win but 1...♔f4 would draw.

D   All roads lead to Rome in that with best play both 1...♔xe4 and 1...♔f4 lead to a draw.

E   White is winning.

A ☐ **B** ☐ **C** ☐ **D** ☐ **E** ☐ **Points**............

Black has just played 14...♘c5 to reach the position below. Is the time right for a sacrifice?

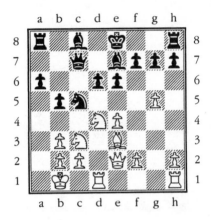

A   Yes. 15 ♘d(or c)xb5 axb5 16 ♘xb5 would pile big time pressure on d6.

B   Yes. 15 ♘d5 should deflect Black's e-pawn to facilitate 16 ♘f5.

C   Yes. 15 ♘f5 should deflect Black's e-pawn to facilitate 16 ♘d5.

D   Yes, but not a piece. 15 g6 is thematic.

E   No. There are some interesting possibilities but there is no need for White to hurry. 15 f4 and 15 b4 are sensible.

A ☐ **B** ☐ **C** ☐ **D** ☐ **E** ☐ **Points**............

It seems like a tall order but can White (on the move) manoeuvre his knight in such a way as to prevent a successful promotion of White's passed h-pawn?

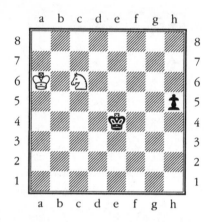

A   No! Providing Black moves his king to the correct square when the need arises, the dangerous outside pawn will reincarnate as a queen.

B   Not really but White can set up a fortress with the king and knight in the a8-corner that will be impenetrable to the black king and queen. Hence White can salvage a draw.

C   Yes via 1 ♘e7.

D   Yes via 1 ♘d8.

E   Yes via 1 ♘a5.

A ☐ **B** ☐ **C** ☐ **D** ☐ **E** ☐ **Points**...........

Black is a piece up but bearing in mind White has a threat or two of his own, can he realistically expect to win?

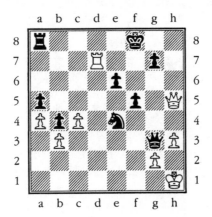

A   Yes with the calm 1...♚g8.

B   Yes by effectively simplifying with 1...♛xh3+.

C   Yes providing he employs his knight (either now or after a repetition) via 1...♘f2+.

D   Yes but it is only 1...♛e1+ that is totally convincing.

E   No, to do anything other than a perpetual check would be asking for trouble when you consider the relative positions of the rooks.

A ☐   **B** ☐   **C** ☐   **D** ☐   **E** ☐   **Points**...........

20 moves into the game White has found himself in possession of the bishop pair. Though he would dearly love to exploit the holes in his opponent's king position, he must first deal with the attack to his queen. Which of the moves below would you prefer?

A   21 ♕h4.

B   21 ♕b4.

C   21 ♕e2.

D   21 ♕e3.

E   21 ♕g4.

A ☐ **B** ☐ **C** ☐ **D** ☐ **E** ☐ **Points**............

What's the truth about this basic king and pawn ending in which it is White to move?

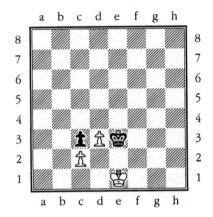

A   1 d4 ♚xd4 (or 1...♚e4 2 ♚e2) 2 ♚f2 is the only way to win.

B   1 ♚d1 is the only way to win.

C   Both 1 d4 and 1 ♚d1 win.

D   1 ♚f1 is the best move.

E   With correct play Black can hold the draw.

A ☐   **B** ☐   **C** ☐   **D** ☐   **E** ☐   **Points**..............

How would you assess the materially imbalanced middlegame in which it is White to play below?

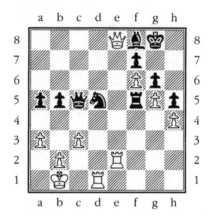

A   Black's position is preferable as a knight and bishop is better than a rook and a pawn.

B   White has a slight plus as his major pieces dominate the vital d- and e-files.

C   Basically White is completely winning.

D   There is a kind of dynamic equilibrium. 'Equal' is a fair assessment.

E   The position is a complete mess and only the likes of Fritz can figure this sort of thing out!

A ☐ **B** ☐ **C** ☐ **D** ☐ **E** ☐ **Points**...........

Can you discern the truth about the tricky ending below in which it is White to move?

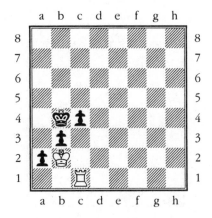

A   White has five moves that hold the draw. They are 1 ♖d1, 1 ♖e1, 1 ♖f1, 1 ♖g1 and 1 ♖h1.

B   1 ♖xc4+ is the best move.

C   1 ♔a1 is the best move.

D   White is lost.

E   White is winning.

A ☐ **B** ☐ **C** ☐ **D** ☐ **E** ☐   **Points**............

With both rooks attacked there are obviously some tactics involved in the endgame below. With Black to play can you get to the bottom of things?

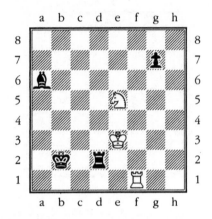

A   1 ♗xf1 is the simplest way for Black to win.

B   Black wins with 1...♖d5.

C   Black wins after 1...♖e2+.

D   White has enough defensive resources to reach a theoretical draw against any winning attempt.

E   Actually it is White who is winning!

A ☐ **B** ☐ **C** ☐ **D** ☐ **E** ☐ **Points**...........

How should Black to move handle the position he finds himself in below?

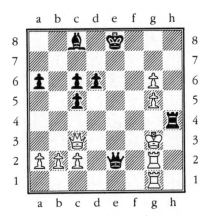

A   He should resign now so as not to prolong his agony!

B   He should resign himself but only to a perpetual check! 1...♖g4+ 2 ♔h2 ♖h4+ is a safe way to achieve just that.

C   He should play on for the win via 1...♕g4+.

D   He should play on for the win via 1...♖h3+.

E   Black can win by employing a move not yet mentioned.

A ☐ **B** ☐ **C** ☐ **D** ☐ **E** ☐ **Points**...........

It's early doors below but as Black what do you think is the best pair of suggestions for how to continue?

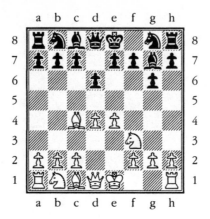

A   With 1...e6 or 1...♞f6.

B   With 1...♞f6 or 1...♞d7.

C   With 1...♞d7 or 1...c6.

D   With 1...c5 or 1...♝g4.

E   With 1...a6 or 1...h5.

A ☐ **B** ☐ **C** ☐ **D** ☐ **E** ☐ **Points**...........

Is there a tactical blow that would work for White in this position?

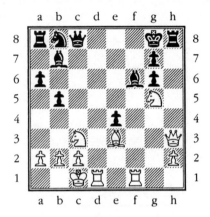

A   Dream on! All of the tactics favour Black who stands better here because of the bishop pair in an open position.

B   Yes, 1 ♕xh8+ is stunning.

C   Yes, 1 ♖d8+ has more punch than Mike Tyson and more bite than, well Mike Tyson!

D   Yes, 1 ♖xf6 will deliver the goods.

E   No! However both 1 ♕xc8+ and 1 ♕g3 look sensible and leave White with the upper hand.

A ☐ **B** ☐ **C** ☐ **D** ☐ **E** ☐ **Points**...........

What is the truth about the interesting endgame below in which Black to move has a possibly critical decision to make?

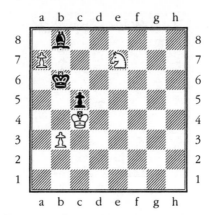

A   Black must force White into an under promotion that will result in a draw because it's not possible to checkmate with two knights.

B   ONLY capturing on a7 with the bishop will draw.

C   ONLY capturing on a7 with the king will draw.

D   Both 1...♗xa7 and 1...♔xa7 draw (with accurate defence obviously!).

E   There is very little critical about this simple ending. White wins whatever.

A ☐ **B** ☐ **C** ☐ **D** ☐ **E** ☐ **Points**............

A fairly straightforward middlegame position with apparently many options for White (to move). Which of the suggestions below would you recommend the first player take?

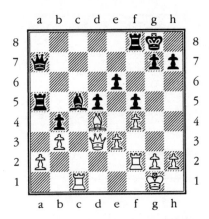

A 1 ♖xc5 with the intention of utilising the d4-a7 pin.

B 1 ♖xc5 ♖xc5 2 ♗xc5 or (1 ♗xc5 ♖xc5 2 ♖xc5) i.e. trading rook and bishop to secure the c-file for the remaining white rook.

C 1 ♖fc2 to dominate the c-file with both rooks.

D 1 ♖cc2 keeping control of the c-file whilst defending the a2-pawn.

E 1 ♖e1 sneakily preparing to target e6 after the inevitable trade of bishops.

A ☐ B ☐ C ☐ D ☐ E ☐ **Points**............

Which of the following statements are true regarding the endgame below in which it is White to move?

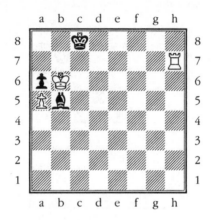

A   White should win with best play.

B   After 1 ♖c7+, only 1...♔b8 draws for Black.

C   After 1 ♖c7+ only 1...♔d8 draws for Black.

D   After 1 ♖c7+ both 1...♔b8 and 1...♔d8 should draw.

E   Endgames are boring!

A □ **B** □ **C** □ **D** □ **E** □ **Points**...........

What is the most accurate move for Black in the position below?

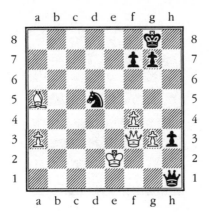

A   1...♛g2+.

B   1...♛xf3+.

C   1...♛h2+.

D   1...♛g1.

E   1...♛b1.

A ☐ **B** ☐ **C** ☐ **D** ☐ **E** ☐ **Points**............

In the position below (with White to move) who is better and why?

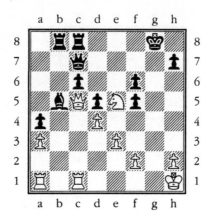

A   White (slightly) because his knight is superior to Black's 'bad' bishop.

B   Black (slightly) because his bishop can help exploit the weak light-squares around the white king.

C   White because he is winning by force.

D   Black because he is winning by force.

E   White's better pawn structure compensates him for his half a pawn deficit. Taking into consideration the bishop for knight issue too and you'd have to say that chances are even.

A ☐ **B** ☐ **C** ☐ **D** ☐ **E** ☐ **Points**...........

It's White to move, what's happening below?

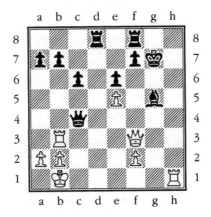

A Black is winning!

B It's a draw!

C After 1 ♕h5 White is winning.

D After 1 ♖g1 White stands better.

E Something other than 1 ♕h5 or 1 ♖g1 wins for White.

A ☐	B ☐	C ☐	D ☐	E ☐	**Points**..........

It's Black to play. What's the story about the realistic rook and pawn ending below?

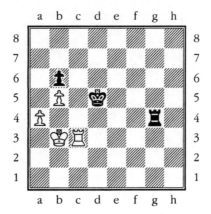

A   As Black has the more centralised king, he stands better!

B   As Black's king is cut off he is lost.

C   Black must play 1...♖g6 to hold the draw.

D   Black can draw and 1...♖h4 looks like a reasonable place to start.

E   All rook and pawn endings are drawn!

A ☐ **B** ☐ **C** ☐ **D** ☐ **E** ☐ **Points**...........

What on earth is going on in the crazy position below in which it is White to move?

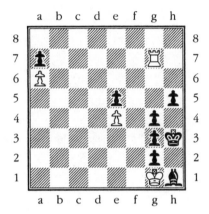

A   Black is winning.

B   White should win after 1 ♖xa7.

C   White should win after 1 ♖b7.

D   Key stalemate ideas save the day for Black. It's a draw.

E   This is outrageous! It's clearly a fabricated position and not the good realistic instructive type of situation that I was expecting when buying this book (or leafing through it at a bookstall!).

A ☐ **B** ☐ **C** ☐ **D** ☐ **E** ☐ **Points**............

How would you assess this more realistic rook and pawn ending below in which it is White to play?

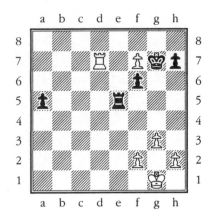

A   White should play 1 f8=♕+ when he should go on to win.

B   White is winning but 1 g4 is a critical move.

C   Best is 1 ♖a7 to get the rook behind the passed pawn. White is winning.

D   1 ♔g2 is the most logical move when White has excellent winning chances.

E   With sensible play Black will be able to hold the draw.

A ☐ **B** ☐ **C** ☐ **D** ☐ **E** ☐ **Points**...........

White has a well-placed knight on f5 and a handy pin on the d-file. With that in mind can you detect the WORST black move of the selection below?

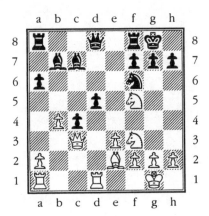

A   1...g6.

B   1...♗c8.

C   1...♖c8.

D   1...♖e8.

E   1...♛e8.

A ☐ **B** ☐ **C** ☐ **D** ☐ **E** ☐   **Points**...........

It's White to play below. What should happen?

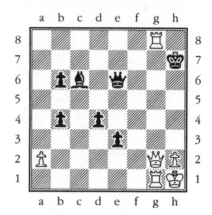

A   White should play 1 ♖h8+ and he will win.

B   White should play 1 ♖g7+ and he will win.

C   There is a move other than 1 ♖h8+ and 1 ♖g7+ that wins for White.

D   With best play it's a draw.

E   Black should win.

A ☐ B ☐ C ☐ D ☐ E ☐ **Points**...........

Which is the most truthful statement about the opening position below in which it is Black to play?

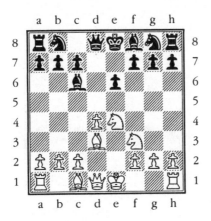

A   1...♘f6 2 ♘xf6+ ♕xf6 is fine for Black but 1...♘d7 2 ♕e2 ♘gf6 3 ♘xf6+ ♕xf6 is not.

B   1...♘d7 2 ♕e2 ♘gf6 3 ♘xf6+ ♕xf6 is fine for Black but 1...♘f6 2 ♘xf6+ ♕xf6 is not.

C   Both 1...♘f6 2 ♘xf6+ ♕xf6 and 1...♘d7 2 ♕e2 ♘gf6 3 ♘xf6+ ♕xf6 are acceptable sequences for Black.

D   Black should steer clear of both 1...♘f6 2 ♘xf6+ ♕xf6 and 1...♘d7 2 ♕e2 ♘gf6 3 ♘xf6+♕xf6 as in both instances Black will lose material.

E   If it's not a Sicilian Dragon, openings don't interest me!

A ☐   B ☐   C ☐   D ☐   E ☐   **Points**............

Which of the alternatives to trading knights on b8 do you find the most attractive in this apparently straightforward middlegame?

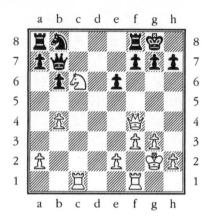

A   1 b5.

B   1 ♘e5.

C   1 ♘d4.

D   1 ♘d8.

E   1 ♘e7+.

A ☐ **B** ☐ **C** ☐ **D** ☐ **E** ☐ **Points**............

Can White (to play) win this seemingly simple king and pawn ending?

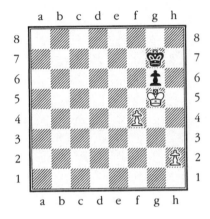

A   Yes if he kicks off with 1 h4.

B   Yes if he kicks off with 1 h3.

C   Yes if 1 f5 is employed.

D   Yes but he must triangulate with his king. 1 ♔g4 is correct.

E   Only if his opponent plays like a lemon. The ending is drawn.

A ☐   B ☐   C ☐   D ☐   E ☐   **Points**...........

It's Black to play in the position below. Do any of the following sacrifices ring your chimes?

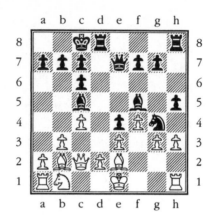

A   Yes 12...♖xd2 gets to the crux of the matter.

B   Yes 12...♘xe3 looks value for money.

C   Yes 12...♗xe3 hits the mark.

D   Yes 12...h4 introduces wicked play on the h-file.

E   Not particularly. 12...♘f6 is sensible and leaves Black with an edge.

A □   **B** □   **C** □   **D** □   **E** □   **Points**...........

What is the most emphatic continuation for White in the position below?

A   1 ♗h6 obviously!

B   Without a doubt 1 ♘xe6.

C   1 ♘f5. How dare you insult my intelligence!

D   1 ♘db5. It wins material.

E   It's not exactly emphatic but 1 ♘xd5 is best.

A ☐	B ☐	C ☐	D ☐	E ☐	Points............

What is the real story about the limited material position below?

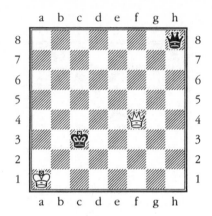

A   If it is White to play he is winning but if it is Black to play it's a draw.

B   If it is Black to play he is winning but if it is White to play it's a draw.

C   Whoever has the move is winning.

D   Whoever is to move Black is winning.

E   The whole situation is very unclear!

A ☐   B ☐   C ☐   D ☐   E ☐   **Points**............

How would you assess the sacrifice 1 ♗xh6 in the middlegame below?

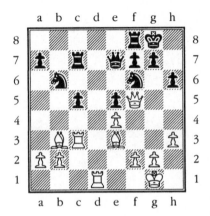

A   Good providing White meets 1...gxh6 with 2 ♖d6.

B   Good providing White meets 1...gxh6 with 2 ♖g3+.

C   Good providing White meets 1...gxh6 with 2 ♕g6+.

D   Rather bad considering the advantage White currently holds.

E   Okay but White would be better off playing a simple move such as 1 ♖dc1.

A ☐   B ☐   C ☐   D ☐   E ☐   **Points**............

Black has two menacing pawns in the endgame below but with White to play can he salvage a draw?

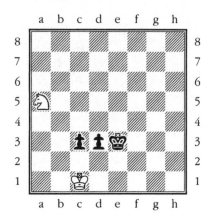

A   Yes via 1 ♘c4+.

B   Yes via 1 ♘b3.

C   Yes via 1 ♘c6.

D   Yes via 1 ♔d1.

E   I'm afraid not. The connected pawns prove too dangerous.

A ☐   **B** ☐   **C** ☐   **D** ☐   **E** ☐   **Points**............

It's White to play in the chaos that is the middlegame below. Can you unravel the tactical complexities and reach a conclusion regarding what on earth is going on?

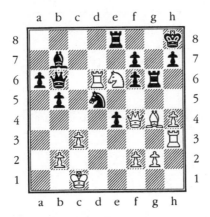

A Do I look like a computer?

B Sure, Black is winning.

C Yes. After a long tactical sequence, approximate equality will be reached.

D Yes it's simple. With the straightforward 27 ♖xb6 White has the upper hand.

E White should win provided he finds a move of utter genius!

A ☐ **B** ☐ **C** ☐ **D** ☐ **E** ☐ **Points**...........

With White to play in both cases, what should be the outcome of this and a similar ending?

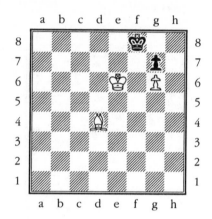

A   This is a draw but White would be winning if the bishop were on d5 instead of d4.

B   This is a White win but it would only be a draw were the bishop on d5 instead of d4.

C   This is a draw as would be the position with the bishop on d5 instead of d4.

D   This is a win as would be the position with the bishop on d5 instead of d4.

E   Can you repeat the question?

A ☐ **B** ☐ **C** ☐ **D** ☐ **E** ☐ **Points**............

Generally speaking it's not such a good idea to activate your king quite as early as White appears to have done in the position below. Black is a queen down though and bearing that in mind, do you think that he will be able to force a win?

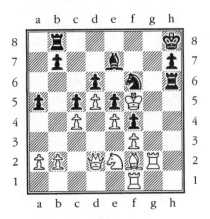

A   No but he has enough for a draw.

B   Yes but only if he kicks off with 33...♘d7.

C   Yes but only if he kicks off with 33...♘g4.

D   Yes. Both 33...♘d7 and 33...♘g4 should win and other knight moves may be good too.

E   No. The material deficiency is too much. White is winning.

A ☐ **B** ☐ **C** ☐ **D** ☐ **E** ☐ **Points**..........

It's Black to play below, what's going down?

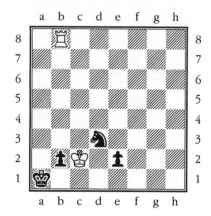

A   Actually White is going down (i.e. losing!) after 1...♘c1.

B   Yep White is going down but only after an under-promotion here and now.

C   He may have the move but in fact Black is lost.

D   With best play it's a draw.

E   I've got a headache!

A ☐ **B** ☐ **C** ☐ **D** ☐ **E** ☐ **Points**............

It's Black to move. Should he win?

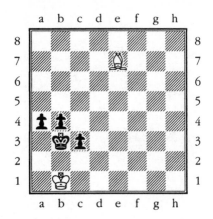

A   Yes but ONLY if he plays 1...a3.

B   Yes but ONLY if he plays 1...c2+.

C   Yes but ONLY if he plays 1...♚c4

D   Yes. In fact any legal move in this position should still lead to a win.

E   No, with careful play White can hold the draw.

A ☐ **B** ☐ **C** ☐ **D** ☐ **E** ☐ **Points**............

Which (if any) of the suggested captures below would offer the best chance to rake in the full point from the position below?

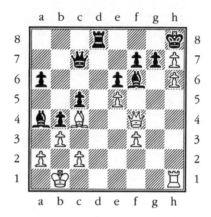

A   1 hxg7+.

B   1 exf6.

C   1 ♕xf6.

D   1 bxa4.

E   None of the above although there is a non-capture that would leave White on the verge of winning.

A ☐	B ☐	C ☐	D ☐	E ☐	**Points**.............

White has a wonderfully dominant bishop pair below but currently on the move, can he realistically expect to be able to win this pawn light endgame?

A   Yes, providing he employs the trade ♗xg8 to perfection.

B   Yes, providing he incorporates the move ♗e5 into his game plan.

C   Yes, providing he goes for checkmate.

D   Yes, providing he utilises the plan of trapping Black's bishop.

E   No. Black's bishop has enough squares to flee to and there is a fortress on the kingside.

A ☐ **B** ☐ **C** ☐ **D** ☐ **E** ☐   **Points**...........

It's decision time for White in the middlegame below. Which route should he take?

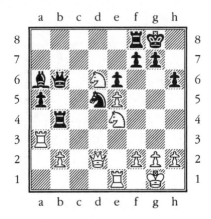

A   1 ♖a2. It is necessary to guard the b-pawn.

B   1 b3. This is the best way to protect the under-fire pawn.

C   1 ♖fa1. Attack is the best form of defence and Black's a-pawn is a natural target.

D   1 ♘f6+. Focusing on the kingside, this is a sacrifice made unashamedly in the quest for mate.

E   1 ♖g3. White should dedicate his resources to a kingside attack.

A ☐ **B** ☐ **C** ☐ **D** ☐ **E** ☐ **Points**............

18 moves into the game, there doesn't seem to be too many tactics flying around below and hence matters are of a more mundane nature. Which of the very reasonable selection of candidate moves would you select for White (to play) in this position?

A   19 b4 to gain space on the queenside and eye up the e5-outpost.

B   19 ♘f4 to hit the black queen and prepare a re-location via d3.

C   19 ♘g3 to offer some cover to the king and vacate the e-file.

D   19 ♗f4 to trade off bad for good bishop and clamp further on e5.

E   19 ♖fe1 to ultimately pressurise Black's backward e-pawn.

A ☐ **B** ☐ **C** ☐ **D** ☐ **E** ☐ **Points**...........

What's going on in the ending below in which it is White to move?

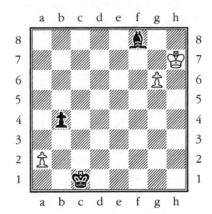

A   White is able to budge the black bishop in order to secure the promotion of his g-pawn. White is winning.

B   Black will ultimately give up his bishop for the passed white g-pawn and then win by taking White's a-pawn and promoting the b-pawn.

C   If winning attempts are exhausted the final position will see two bare kings remaining and a draw declared.

D   If winning attempts are exhausted the final position will see a bare white king and a black king and bishop remaining. A draw will be declared.

E   It could go either way!

A ☐ **B** ☐ **C** ☐ **D** ☐ **E** ☐ **Points**...........

Arguably not the most realistic situation but an interesting test nonetheless. It's White to play, what should happen?

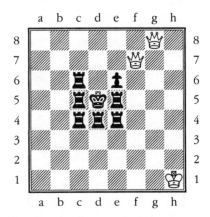

A   1 ♕d8+ is best. If Black refuses a draw offer White will eventually be able to legally claim a draw by threefold repetition of position.

B   White can deliver checkmate in 21 moves.

C   1 ♕xe6+ and White can force a draw.

D   1 ♕b7 and the game should end in a draw.

E   Eventually White's checks dry up. Black is winning.

A ☐   **B** ☐   **C** ☐   **D** ☐   **E** ☐   **Points**...........

Having a 1pt material advantage Black is going for a win in the endgame below. With that in mind what is his best practical continuation?

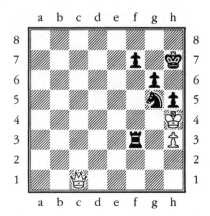

A   70...♖f5.

B   70...♖xh3+.

C   70...♘xh3.

D   70...f6.

E   70...♘e6.

A ☐ B ☐ C ☐ D ☐ E ☐ **Points**...........

*The game has moved on (to move 115 no less!) from our last
position. It's White to play. What should happen now?*

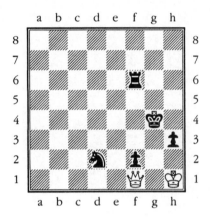

A It seems amazing but White should win!

B White should play 115 ♕e2+ and he will draw.

C White should play 115 ♕d1+ and he will draw.

D White should play something other than 115 ♕e2+ or
115 ♕d1+ in order to draw.

E White has a few tricks but with accurate play Black should
win.

A ☐ **B** ☐ **C** ☐ **D** ☐ **E** ☐ **Points**............

Four moves into the game below, Black appears to be pressurising the d4-pawn big time. How should White handle this situation?

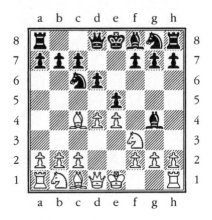

A   By resolving the tension in the centre; 5 dxe5.

B   By advancing the under-fire pawn; 5 d5.

C   By offering support from a compatriot; 5 c3.

D   Black can be punished elsewhere; 5 ♘xe5.

E   Black can be punished elsewhere; 5 ♗xf7+.

A ☐ **B** ☐ **C** ☐ **D** ☐ **E** ☐ **Points**............

Though a couple of pawns down, White's remaining pieces are as actively placed as they could realistically be in the position below. How would you recommend he turn up the heat?

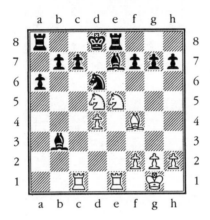

A With 1 ♘xf7+. It's stunning!

B With 1 ♘xc7 forking the black rooks.

C With 1 ♖xc7 invading the 7th rank.

D With the crafty 1 ♘b4 eyeing up the c6-square.

E With 1 ♘xe7; simple chess!

A ☐ B ☐ C ☐ D ☐ E ☐ Points...........

It's White to play in the endgame below. What should happen?

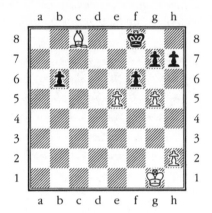

A   1 exf6 gxf6 2 gxf6 (or 1 gxf6 gxf6 2 exf6) and White will win.

B   1 gxf6 gxf6 2 e6 and White will win.

C   1 ♗f5 and White will win.

D   Black will be able to hold the draw.

E   Black will win!

A ☐   **B** ☐   **C** ☐   **D** ☐   **E** ☐   **Points**...........

How are things shaping up for Black (to play) in the king and pawn ending below?

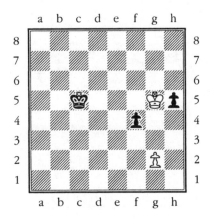

A   Pretty grim! He is lost.

B   Okay. He can draw with 1...♚d4.

C   Not bad. He can draw with 1...♚d6.

D   Alright as 1...h4 saves the day.

E   So so, as 1...f3 salvages a half point.

A ☐ **B** ☐ **C** ☐ **D** ☐ **E** ☐ **Points**............

Which of the following statements is the most accurate regarding the possibility of the move 3 ♘xe5 for White in the opening position below?

A   Highly recommended it bags at least a pawn, objectively leaving White with a winning position.

B   It's a very reasonable move which will lead to a positional advantage. On the other hand there are other good moves to be found here too.

C   3 ♘xe5 is not especially good as Black can equalise fairly easily.

D   It is a very bad idea. Frankly 2...f6 is ridiculous but it does set one trap and 3 ♘xe5? walks straight into it.

E   Oh I see, another opening question. That's it I've had enough, I'm outta here!

A ☐ **B** ☐ **C** ☐ **D** ☐ **E** ☐ **Points**...........

Clearly it's White to play below. Get that analysing cap on and figure out whether White will be able to prevent Black from getting a perpetual check (i.e. without walking into a mating net!).

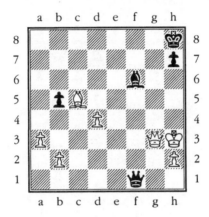

A   Not providing Black checks on all the right squares.

B   Yes, after 1 ♕g2 White will eventually be able to negotiate a safe haven for his king.

C   Yes but only if 1 ♔g4 is employed.

D   Actually a draw would be an exceptionally good result for White here as Black can in fact win by force.

E   It depends on who it is to move!

A ☐ **B** ☐ **C** ☐ **D** ☐ **E** ☐ **Points**............

Black has a pretty solid 'Hedgehog' style set-up in the middlegame below. It is White to play though and your test is to uncover the lemon (i.e. the move not to be recommended!) in the list of the following candidate moves.

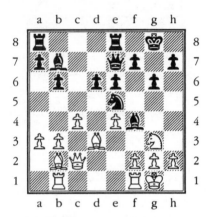

A   1 ♖bd1 to place a rook on a half-open file.

B   1 ♖fe1 to centralise a rook and attempt to dissuade the future break ...d5.

C   1 ♘e2 to try and budge the bishop and thus prepare f2-f4.

D   1 ♗e2 to preserve the bishop pair.

E   1 a4 to begin making inroads on the queenside.

A ☐   **B** ☐   **C** ☐   **D** ☐   **E** ☐   **Points**...........

Below is a typically sharp Open Sicilian middlegame position. How should White deal with the dual attack to his two bishops?

A   With 1 ♗c6+ winning a significant amount of material.

B   With the straightforward 1 ♗xb7, leading to a comfortably better endgame.

C   With the stunning 1 ♘f5. The black king will be caught in a crossfire.

D   With the devastating sacrifice 1 ♘xe6.

E   Via the cautious 1 ♘f3 keeping everything under control.

A ☐	B ☐	C ☐	D ☐	E ☐	**Points**...........

What's the truth about the ending below in which it is White to play?

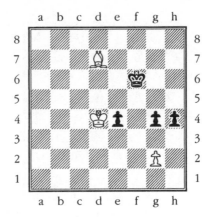

A   White should win after 1 ♔xe4.

B   White should win after 1 ♔e3.

C   White should win after 1 ♗c6.

D   White should win after 1 ♗xg4.

E   With precise play Black can hold the draw.

A ☐ **B** ☐ **C** ☐ **D** ☐ **E** ☐ **Points**............

Can you spot the only correct statement regarding the following king and pawn ending in which it is White to play?

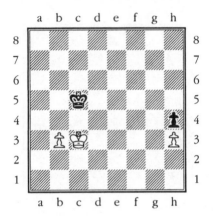

A Were the h-pawns not present White would be winning because he has the opposition.

B White wins by racing his king over to the kingside.

C After 1 b4+ White will win by simple means.

D In order to win White must triangulate with his king.

E It's a draw!

A ☐ B ☐ C ☐ D ☐ E ☐ **Points**............

On the move in the position below White is contemplating grabbing the unprotected pawn on a7. Should he take it?

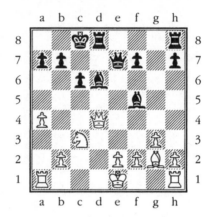

A   No. King safety should be a priority and hence 1 0-0 is best.

B   No. White should focus more on completing his development and 1 0-0-0 kills two birds with one stone.

C   No. 1 ♗e4 centralising the bishop and seeking to break up Black's bishop pair is a far superior move.

D   No. 1 a5 offers a niche for the queen and that is the piece that White should be concerned about right now.

E   Yes! A pawn is a pawn and on a7 the queen will be a real thorn in the black position.

A ☐ **B** ☐ **C** ☐ **D** ☐ **E** ☐ **Points**...........

Currently having the move, is White winning this perfectly feasible king, knight and pawn versus bare king scenario below?

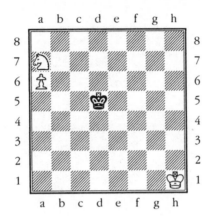

A   Yes but ONLY if he begins with 1 ♘c8.

B   Yes but ONLY if he begins with 1 ♘b5.

C   Yes but ONLY if he starts with a king move.

D   Yes, in fact any move EXCEPT 1 ♘c6 would win.

E   No. Black can force a drawn position.

A ☐   **B** ☐   **C** ☐   **D** ☐   **E** ☐   **Points**...........

Could it be that the outcome of the bishop endgame below depends upon who is to move?

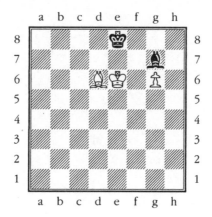

A   Absolutely! With White to play he wins via 1 ♗e5 but with Black to play it's a draw.

B   Yes. Black is lost if it is his move but if it isn't then he should draw.

C   No. This is a theoretical draw whoever is to move.

D   No. It doesn't matter whose turn it is to move, Black is lost.

E   It depends on which way the pawn is going!

A ☐ **B** ☐ **C** ☐ **D** ☐ **E** ☐ **Points**...........

Black to play is considering the tactic 1...♘g3+ in the position below? What advice might you offer him?

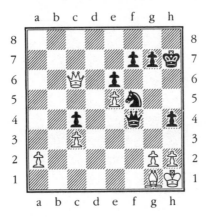

A Go for it! It most surely wins by force.

B It is worth a go. Black will reach a favourable queen ending although it is far from clear that the full point is guaranteed.

C Don't do it. Instead 1...h3 will expose the black king in the desired manner.

D With all things considered, it is not the best move. Black should turn the screws slowly and 1...♔g6 looks more sensible.

E You should never offer advice to anyone during a game whatever language those words of wisdom might be spoken in! I'm reporting anyone that chose A-D to the appropriate authorities!

A ☐ **B** ☐ **C** ☐ **D** ☐ **E** ☐ **Points**...........

Does it matter who is to play in the simple looking king and pawn ending below?

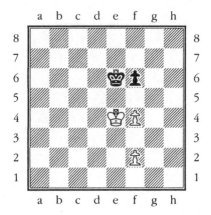

A   Yes as this is a position of 'mutual zugzwang'. If it is Black to play he loses but if it is White to play he draws.

B   Yes. Black to play can draw with 1...f5+ but White wins if it his turn.

C   No. It is a draw whoever has the move.

D   No. It may not look all that, but in fact White's extra pawn is invaluable. He wins whoever it is to play.

E   Ah yes this is one of those puzzles that involves triangulating the distant opposition in order to match the related squares and push off the king from the recommended defensive set-up in order to under-promote. The answer is categorically "yes", er and "no"! Um what exactly was the question again?

A ☐ **B** ☐ **C** ☐ **D** ☐ **E** ☐ **Points**...........

Not entirely unrelated to the last question(!), can you conclude whether White (to play) is winning?

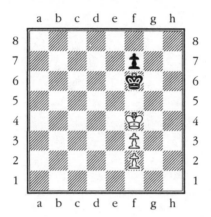

A   It is impossible to come to any conclusion without being in full possession of all of the facts!

B   Yes he is for example winning after the sequence 1 ♔e4 ♚e6 2 f4 f6.

C   Yes he is for example winning after the sequence 1 ♔g4 ♚g6 2 f4 f6.

D   No, far from it. Black has the opposition and it is he who is winning.

E   No. With careful defence Black can rebuff all winning attempts.

A ☐ **B** ☐ **C** ☐ **D** ☐ **E** ☐ **Points**...........

Is it a capture that is the best move for Black (to play) in the middlegame below?

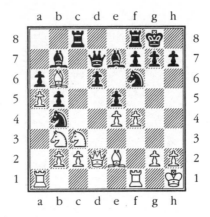

A   Yes 1...♘xe4 opens up the long diagonal and will leave Black with compensation for the material sacrificed.

B   Yes 1...♗xe4 will ultimately leave a black knight dangerously placed in the centre of the board.

C   Yes 1...♖xc3 is a typical Sicilian exchange sacrifice that works a treat here.

D   Yes, before White's f-pawn advances further, 1...exf4 is correct to secure Black the use of the e5-square.

E   No. Tempting though some of them may be, the correct course of action here is the thematic break in the centre 1...d5.

A ☐ **B** ☐ **C** ☐ **D** ☐ **E** ☐ **Points**...........

Just 6 moves into the game Black is considering mixing things up with 6...e4. What have you got to say on the matter?

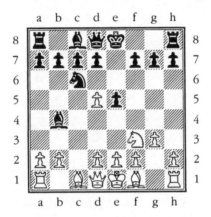

A   It looks quite interesting and under the circumstances is definitely worth a punt!

B   Don't do it! 6...e4 practically loses by force.

C   It would lead to a slightly worse position. 6...♘e7 would be better.

D   It's slightly inferior to the best move which is 6...♘d4.

E   No. Black must opt for 6...♘b8.

A ☐ **B** ☐ **C** ☐ **D** ☐ **E** ☐ **Points**...........

I can tell you that an unnamed computer analysis module believes that despite it being White's move, Black is winning the position below. What do you think?

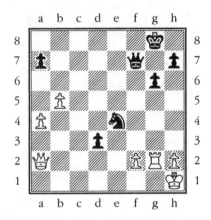

A   Frankly that is a lucky guess! Black is winning but there are plenty of twists and turns in the main variation.

B   Black is winning if White trades queens but if White preserves them now then he is not worse.

C   Wrong because 1 f3 saves the day. Actually White is winning.

D   Wrong! After 1 ♕xf7 it is White who stands better.

E   The computer is wrong. With best play it is a draw.

A ☐ **B** ☐ **C** ☐ **D** ☐ **E** ☐ **Points**...........

Arguably a subjective question, as Black to play below, how would you deal with threat to the light-squared bishop?

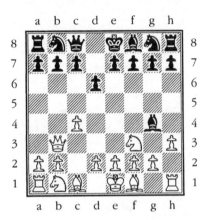

A   What threat?

B   With 1...♗h5 retaining the bishop but maintaining the pressure on f3.

C   With 1...♗f5 retreating to a fairly useful diagonal.

D   With 1...♗d7 intending to re-locate the bishop on c6 and develop the queen's knight on d7.

E   With 1...♗xf3. Perhaps it's not ideal to concede a bishop for a knight so early but it is better than the alternatives.

A ☐   **B** ☐   **C** ☐   **D** ☐   **E** ☐   **Points**...........

Is there a successful winning plan that White (to play) can employ to convert the two pawns advantage into a full point in the endgame below?

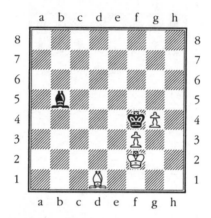

A   Yes. He should sacrifice his g-pawn now with 1 g5 in order to pave the way for his f-pawn to move up the board.

B   Yes. He must simply trade off bishops to reach a king and pawn endgame. That of course would be trivial.

C   Yes. Starting with 1 ♔g2 he should bring his king up into action via the h-file.

D   Yes. Starting with 1 ♔e1 he should bring his king the long way round. Penetrating via the centre the white monarch will eventually be able to assist the advance of the pawns.

E   No and it serves him right for putting both pawns on the same colour as his bishop!

A ☐ **B** ☐ **C** ☐ **D** ☐ **E** ☐ **Points**...........

It's White to play below. Do any of the proposed sacrifices take your fancy?

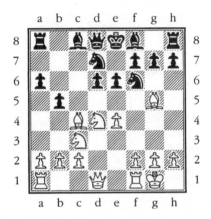

A   Yes 1 ♘xe6 gets to the crux of the matter.

B   Yes 1 ♗xe6 is a tasty morsel!

C   Yes 1 ♘dxb5 deals with a threat and creates a threat.

D   No. 1 ♗b3 is normal.

E   I suppose "yes" and "no" is the answer. 1 ♘c6 is the strongest move.

A ☐ **B** ☐ **C** ☐ **D** ☐ **E** ☐ **Points**...........

Is there a good sacrifice for White (to play) in this position?

A White should just castle now to complete his development!

B Yes 1 ♗xf7 is crushing.

C Yes 1 ♗xg5 looks good.

D Yes 1 ♘xg5 is promising.

E No. Simple chess is best here and that means 1 ♗g3.

A ☐ **B** ☐ **C** ☐ **D** ☐ **E** ☐ **Points**...........

In the position below, can Black get away with grabbing the a2-pawn?

A   Yes 1...♛xa2 looks like a sound sacrifice.

B   Yes and he definitely should because after 1...♞xa2+, White's attention must be focused on his own king.

C   1...♞xa2 is okay but 1...♝g7 would be more shrewd.

D   1...♞xa2 is okay but 1...♝e6 would be a better bet.

E   Absolutely not! Black's position isn't great but 1...c5 should keep him in the game.

A ☐ **B** ☐ **C** ☐ **D** ☐ **E** ☐ **Points**...........

What do you think is the most accurate assessment of the position below in which it is White to play?

A   After 1 ♕e2 White should enter a slightly better endgame.

B   After 1 ♕g4 White should enter a slightly better endgame.

C   Overall the position is fairly equal.

D   White is winning.

E   Black has a slight advantage.

A ☐ **B** ☐ **C** ☐ **D** ☐ **E** ☐ **Points**............

It's Black to play in the tense middlegame below. Which move do you think stands out as the most precise amongst the other candidate moves?

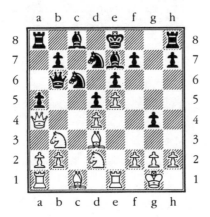

A   1...h5.

B   1...f5.

C   1...♛b4.

D   1...♛c7.

E   1...0-0.

A ☐ **B** ☐ **C** ☐ **D** ☐ **E** ☐ **Points**............

Can Black get away with 1...♛xd4 in the position below?

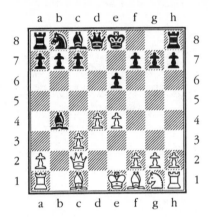

A   No but only because of 1 ♕a4+ ultimately obtaining a very good ending for White.

B   No but ONLY because of 1 ♗d2 leaving the bishop and queen forked.

C   No but ONLY because of 1 ♗b2 leaving the bishop and queen forked.

D   No in view of both 1 ♗d2 and 1 ♗b2.

E   Yes and under the circumstances it is most certainly the best move.

A □ **B** □ **C** □ **D** □ **E** □ **Points**...........

Regarding the king and pawn endgame below in which it is White to play, try to discover the only truism.

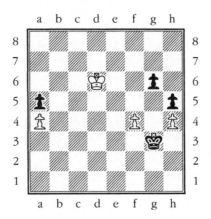

A   After 1 ♔c5 White is winning.

B   After 1 ♔c5 the game should end in a draw.

C   After 1 ♔d5 White should draw.

D   After 1 ♔e5 Black should reach a very favourable queen ending but White should draw.

E   Black is winning.

A ☐ **B** ☐ **C** ☐ **D** ☐ **E** ☐ **Points**............

Referring to the endgame below in which it White to move, please uncover the only truthful statement amongst the other falsehoods.

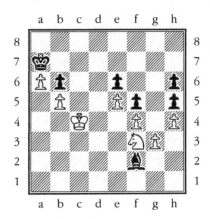

A   Although there is still plenty of play left, as things are so blocked up, a draw is inevitable.

B   White's kingside pawns are for the chop. Black is winning.

C   1 ♘d4 is the best move.

D   White is winning.

E   Strictly speaking, none of the above statements are true.

A ☐ B ☐ C ☐ D ☐ E ☐ **Points**...........

Which of the candidate moves for White (to play in the position below) would you eliminate straight away (i.e. which is the WORST)?

A   1 ♗f4.

B   1 ♗g5.

C   1 0-0.

D   1 f3.

E   1 ♕b3.

A ☐ **B** ☐ **C** ☐ **D** ☐ **E** ☐ **Points**...........

The position below was reached recently in a game between two strong Grandmasters. In your opinion what is the best move for White?

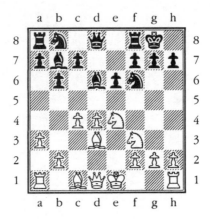

A   1 ♘g3.

B   1 ♕e2.

C   1 ♘xf6+.

D   1 ♘xd6.

E   1 ♕e2.

A ☐ **B** ☐ **C** ☐ **D** ☐ **E** ☐ **Points**...........

Test One: Answers

Q1

No doubt if I had asked "How can White win" then most would surely have observed the stunning 1 ♕a8!!, as played in Paglilla-Carbone, Argentina, 1985.

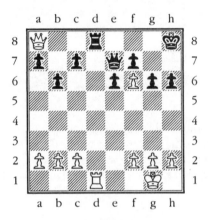

The point is of course that Black doesn't get to flick in the back rank mate as his own king is pinned. His own queen remains attacked and after 1...♖xa8 2 fxe7, next up is 3 ♖d8+. 5 pts for **D**.

Regarding my first observation, this is not that type of book and (just as in a real game) there is nobody here to give you clues!

Q2

First of all I'd like to think that you easily eliminated options C and D! That aside though this is actually a fairly tricky one and the reader could be forgiven for accepting a possible continuation of 1 ♕b7+ ♔c2 2 ♕a6 ♔b2 3 ♕b5+ ♔c2 4 ♕a4+ ♔b2 5 ♕b4+ ♔c2 6 ♕a3 ♔b1 7 ♕b3+ ♔a1 8 ♕c2 with mate on c1 following next.

As I'm sure that you will remember from *Chess Choice Challenge 1* or other endgame texts, a queen vs a rook's pawn on the 7th is a draw if the defending king is up there with the pawn and the attacker's king is too far away.

In fact with the emphasis on not granting the queen access to the b4-square, Black can instead improve significantly with 3...♔a3! 4 ♕d3+ ♔b2 5 ♕d4+ ♔b3 6 ♔g7 h4 7 ♔f6 h3 8 ♔e5 h2 9 ♕a1 h1=♕ 10 ♕xh1 ♔b2.

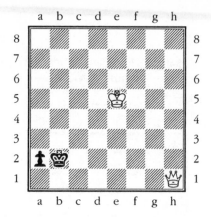

With the white monarch starting so far away the h-pawn was able to offload itself in time in order to reach the above thematic draw. You may also recall situations in which the attacker can win even after allowing the pawn to promote. This isn't one of them! 5 pts for **B**.

Q3

Essentially the justification for the award of 5 pts for **E** comes from the same deflection theme as in question 1. It is a recurring theme and the following is quite beautiful:

Adams – Torre
New Orleans 1920

18 ♕g4!! **♕b5** (The big idea of course is 18...♕xg4 19 ♖xe8+ ♖xe8 20 ♖xe8 mate. As the knight guards e1, there is no time to take the rook on e2.) **19 ♕c4!!** **♕d7** (Still the white queen is out of bounds.) **20 ♕c7!!** **♕b5** (Or 20...♕a4 21 b3 ♕b5 22 a4) **21 a4!!** **♕xa4 22 ♖e4!!** **♕b5** (Note that White nets a rook after 22...♖f8 23 ♕xc8! ♕xe4 24 ♕xf8+.) **23 ♕xb7!**

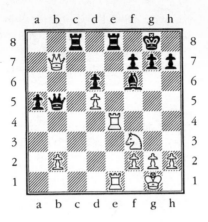

1-0 The black queen has no safe way of continuing to guard e8.

It goes without saying that the bishop vs knight debate was a bit of a red herring here. Sorry about that! Oh alright 2pts for those that selected A.

Q4

Actually it would be an amazing coincidence if you did come across this position as this is exactly what was reached over forty years ago:

Ciocaltea – Fischer
Varna 1962

67...h3+ (Or 67...♖d8 68 b8=♕ h3+ 69 ♔f1 and there is nothing doing.)

68 ♔f1 (I don't see why 68 ♔h1 shouldn't win either and all White need do is avoid 68 ♔g1?? ♖e8! (threatening 69...♖e1 mate) 69 ♖a1 h2+ 70 ♔g2 (or 70 ♔h1 ♔h3) 70...♖e2+ 71 ♔h1 ♔h3 72 ♖g1 hxg1=♕+ 73 ♔xg1 ♖e1 mate.) **68...g2+ 69 ♖xg2+** (Actually 69 ♔g1 was also adequate e.g. 69...♖d8 70 ♖a1 ♔g3 71 b8=♕+ and so it wasn't that difficult a puzzle after all!) **1-0**

There is certainly no evidence to support A and you didn't really think I would award any points for E did you? Well if so, you were wrong and the 5pts go to **B**.

Q5

Well I'm not sure exactly where 1 h4 jumped out from but it certainly wasn't the 'good move guide'! That sort of wing play can hardly be justified whilst the development is incomplete. Mind you, 1 ♖e1 is 'moving' a piece rather than 'developing' one as the rook doesn't do a lot there. I still believe that not thinking of one's rooks is the most popular sin amongst weaker club players and I am all for the planning of pawn breaks. Unfortunately now is not the time for 1 f4?. White would leave himself with an isolated pawn after 1...exf4 2 ♗xf4 and aside from the obvious drawback of having freed Black's dark-squared bishop, Black can bag a pawn immediately via 2...♕d4+. I'm going to award 2pts for A but although one should always bear in mind that useful opening adage 'Knights on the rim are dim!', the flexibility that earns **B** the maximum 5pts is superbly highlighted in the following instructive encounter:

Stean – Planinc
Moscow 1975

1...♘a3 (Aiming for c4, this knight has the weak squares b6 and d6 in its sights as well as the black pawn on e5.) **12...♗e6 13 ♘ac4 ♗xc4 14 ♗xc4** (The bishop for knight gain is a significant break-through.) **14...♕d7 15 f3 ♘h5 16 g3** (Keeping the black knight out of f4. White also has no desire to see Black's bishop activated.) **16...♖ad8 17 ♗b3!** (White intends a repeat performance with the c4-square being vacated for the use of the other white steed.). **17...c5 18 ♕e2 b6 19 ♖fd1 ♕c7 20 c3 ♘c6 21 ♘c4 ♘f6 22 ♘a3! ♘a7 23 ♕c4 ♖fe8 24 ♔g2 h6 25 ♖xd8 ♖xd8 26 ♖d1 ♖xd1 27 ♗xd1 ♗f8 28 ♗e2 ♔g7 29 ♕b3 ♘e8 30 ♗a6! ♘d6 31 ♕d5! ♘e8 32 ♘c4**

92

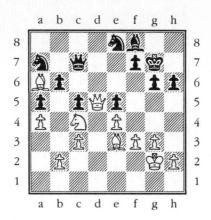

32...♘f6 (White's position has slowly gained in momentum and one tactic does enter the equation: 32...f6 33 ♘xb6! ♕xb6 34 ♗c4 ♕xb2+ 35 ♔h3 and there is no stopping the mate via ♕g8. Presumably Black felt he was too passive after 32...♗d6 33 ♕a8! and so he chooses to offload a pawn. He has insufficient play though and things continue to go according to plan.) **33 ♕xe5 ♕d8 34 ♗f2 g5 35 ♗b7 ♔h8 36 ♗d5 ♔g8 37 ♕f5 1-0**

With a horrendously passive position, there is little that Black can do about ♘e5.

Q6

This test position was reached after 57 ♔b5 in the recent encounter:

Ward – McShane
Copenhagen 2003.

I guess that I was expecting 57...♔xe4 58 ♔xb6 f5 (Not 58...♔f4?? 59 b5 ♔xg4 60 ♔c5 when White will promote but Black won't!) 59 gxf5 ♔xf5 60 b5 g4 61 ♔c6 g3 62 b6 g2 63 b7 g1=♕ 64 b8=♕ and a draw but the game continued in a different way:

57...♔f4 58 ♔xb6 ♔xg4 59 b5 ♔f3 60 ♔c6 (It is sensible not to allow Black to queen with check.) **60...g4 61 e5!**

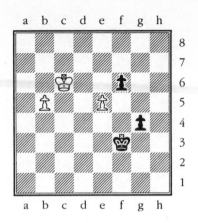

(The simplest way to secure a share of the wares. Instead 61 b6 g3 62 b7 g2 63 b8=♕ g1=♕ should of course still be a draw but White may still have a little work to do.) **61...fxe5** (In view of 61...g3 62 exf6 g2 63 f7 g1=♕ 64 f8=♕+ clearly this pawn cannot be ignored.) **62 b6 g3 63 b7 g2 64 b8=♕ g1=♕ 65 ♕xe5 ½-½**

You should be ashamed of yourself if you opted for A, which isn't the opposition anyway! The 5 pts clearly go to the selection of **D**.

Q7

The answer A is of course garbage as 16...♕a5 would leave White the one in serious danger of being mated. D isn't too impressive in this situation and as Black's bishop looks over the f5-square it is **C** (5 pts) that gets the nod over B. The following is an extremely instructive encounter for Open Sicilian exponents to take note of:

Tseitlin – Zilberstein
USSR 1967

15 ♘f5! exf5 16 ♘d5 ♕b7 17 ♗xc5 dxc5 18 exf5 ♗xf5 (Black had to remove this pawn before it advanced again and he also needs to prepare a defence to ♖he1.) **19 ♕e5!**

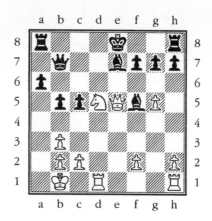

(Queens love it in the centre. From here it hits g7, f5 and of course introduces the threat of ♘c7+. What I love about this sequence is the way that computer analysis engines slowly change their tune from their standard materialistic viewpoint!) **19...♗e6 20 ♘c7+ ♚f8 21 ♘xa8 ♛xa8 22 f4!** (This pawn is raring to march up to f6.) **22...♗g4 23 ♖he1! ♛e8** (Both 23...♛b7? 24 ♖d8+! and 23...♗xd1? 24 ♛xe7+ ♚g8 25 ♛e8+ lead to mate.) **24 ♖d6!** (Smooth! There is no defence to what follows.) **24...♗d7 25 ♖b6! f6 26 gxf6 gxf6 27 ♖xf6+ ♗xf6 28 ♛xf6+ ♚g8 29 ♖g1+ 1-0**

Go on then, 2 pts to the selection of E with the preference being for 15 b4.

Q8

B is the biggest load of drivel I've ever written (!) and the most obvious answer must surely be A (You can very generously have 1pt for that even though let's face it, it is the wrong answer!) as knights are notoriously bad at halting passed rook's pawns. Let's check out the options in order though:

1 ♘e7 h4 2 ♘g6 h3 and the knight is in No Man's Land;

1 ♘d8 h4 2 ♘e6 ♚f5! 3 ♘d4+ ♚g4 4 ♘c2 and now not 4...h3 5 ♘e3+ ♚f3 6 ♘f1 letting the knight onto the relevant track but rather 4...♚f4! when the king dominates the knight.

Yep things aren't looking good until we see:

95

1 ♘a5!! h4 2 ♘c4 ♔f3!? (If 2...h3 then 3 ♘d2+ and White re-aches a well known drawing theme. i.e. 3...♔e3 4 ♘f1+ ♔f2 5 ♘h2 ♔g2 6 ♘g4 ♔g3 7 ♘e3 intending 7...h2 8 ♘f1+.) **3 ♘e5+!** (White must continue to play accurately. Note 3 ♘d2+? ♔e2! 4 ♘e4 h3 5 ♘g3+ ♔f2 and White loses as he was unable to get within range of the h2-square.) **3...♔g3 4 ♘c4 h3 5 ♘e3**

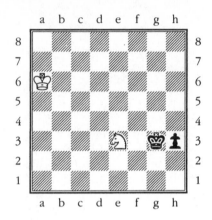

Black can't prevent the knight from getting to either f1 or g4. Truly amazing!

The 5pts go to **E**.

Q9

1...♔g8 is hardly a winning attempt in view of the perpetual 2 ♕f7+ ♔h8 3 ♕h5+ etc. Instead Black can reach a rook ending via 1...♕xh3+ 2 ♕xh3 ♘f2+ 3 ♔h2 ♘xh3 4 ♔xh3 or (probably better) 1...♘f2+ 2 ♔g1 ♘xh3+ 3 ♕xh3 ♕xh3 4 gxh3.

They are far from clear though unlike:

Jedynak – Sapis
Poland 2003

1...♕e1+ 2 ♔h2 ♕h1+!

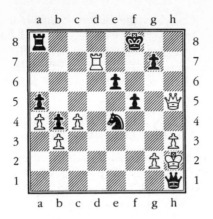

0-1

Cute! After 2...♕h1+ 3 ♔xh1 ♘g3+ 4 ♔h2 ♘xh5, Black will have traded off queens but without losing his knight.

Those who chose **D** get 5pts.

Q10

The following recent practical encounter should be a warning to those who don't guard against over optimism!:

Landa – Potkin
Russian Champs 2003

21 ♕h4?? ♖xd3 22 ♕xe7 ♖g3!

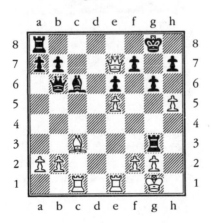

(Pin City Arizona! Critically the f-pawn is unable to move and so its compatriot on g2 is in serious trouble.) **23 ♕h4 ♖xg2+ 24 ♔f1 ♕b5+ 25 ♖e2 ♗f3** (I suspect that with 21 ♕h4 White was hopeful of punishing White on the dark squares. Ironically it is he who suffers, only it is the light squares that are his downfall.) **26 ♖cc2 ♖g4 27 ♕f6 ♗xe2+ 28 ♖xe2 ♖e4 0-1**

Clearly then A is not the solution and neither can be B as 21 ♕b4?? ♖xd3 22 ♕xe7 ♖g3 is merely a transposition.

21 ♕g4?? ♖xd3 is obviously just a blunder as well and that just leaves us with 21 ♕e3 ♕xe3 22 ♖xe3 ♘d5 which is equal at best and the cautious 21 ♕e2 which retains a slight edge. Hey, this book is real life, not fantasy! Of the alternatives given it is C that earns the 5pts.

Q11

Surely this was money for old rope!? The key thing to observe is that:

1 d4 ♔xd4 2 ♔f2 ♔c4 3 ♔e3 ♔c5 4 ♔d3 ♔d5 5 ♔xc3 ♔c5

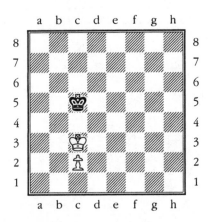

is only a draw because Black retains the opposition.

As 1 ♔f1 ♔d2 2 d4 ♔xc2 3 d5 ♔b2 4 d6 c2 5 d7 c1=♕+ isn't too advisable(!), that just leaves the trivial 1 ♔d1 ♔f3 2 ♔c1 ♔e3 3 ♔b1 ♔d4 4 ♔a2 ♔c5 5 ♔b3 ♔d4 6 ♔b4 when White nets Black's other pawn too.

The answer then is **B** for 5pts.

Q12

Okay I must confess to feeling a bit mean about this one!

In **Apicella – Guidarelli**, French Champs 2003 rather terminal was:

45 ♖e7!! (a quite beautiful example of interference)

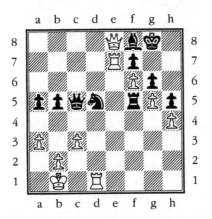

1-0
(In view of 45...♘xe7 46 ♕xf8+!! ♔xf8 (or 46...♔h7 47 ♕g7 mate) 47 ♖d8 mate.)

The easy solution of **C** (5pts) has saved me having to talk about why usually two minor pieces are better than a rook and a pawn in middlegames. Oops I have just talked about it!

Q13

Taking a look at a few variations we have:

1 ♖h1 c3+ 2 ♔a1 ♔a3 and there is no defence to the threat of 3...b2+;
  1 ♖d1 c3+ 2 ♔a1 ♔a3 which is of course no different;
  1 ♖xc4+ ♔xc4 2 ♔a1 ♔b4 3 ♔b2 a1=♕+! 4 ♔xa1 ♔a3 5 ♔b1 b2 6 ♔c2 ♔a2 and the b-pawn will promote;
  1 ♔a1! ♔a3 2 ♖c3

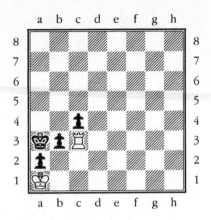

(Pinning the b-pawn.) 2...♔b4 3 ♖c1 c3 4 ♖xc3 ½-½ (It's stale-mate after 4...♔xc3.).

As there is certainly no way for White to win it has to be 5pts for **C**.

Q14

I'll assume that you were able to eliminate E from your enquiries and 1...♗xf1 2 ♔xd2 (when the black king is too far away to aid in the advance of the g-pawn) shouldn't have been too difficult to assess as an easy draw.

White also avoids the loss of material after 1...♖d5 2 ♖f5 and that just leaves one critical variation:

1...♖e2+ 2 ♔d4 (After 2 ♔f4? ♖xe5 White doesn't have the same brilliant possibility as in the main line.) **2...♖xe5 3 ♖f6!!**

(The work of a genius. The previously attacked white rook hits the black bishop on a square where it can't be taken because of stalemate.) **3...♖a5 4 ♖g6.**

White picks up the g-pawn resulting in a theoretically drawn rook and bishop versus rook scenario. Okay there will still be some accurate defending to do (so actually I'm giving 2pts for C) but nevertheless it can be concluded that **D** is spot on.

Q15

This puzzle was taken from the game Stoltz – Pilnik, Saltsjobaden 1952 which concluded 1...♖g4+ 2 ♔h2 ♖h4+ 3 ♔g3 i.e. a draw by perpetual check.

Definitely an inferior try is 1...♕g4+ e.g. 2 ♔f2 ♕f4+ 3 ♕f3 ♕d2+ 4 ♕e2+ but the hat must come off to:

1...♖h3+ 2 ♔f4

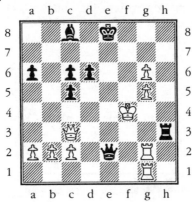

2...♖f3+!! 3 ♕xf3 ♕e5 mate

The correct answer of **D** (5pts) was presumably overlooked!

Q16

In my opinion (which as I'm awarding the points is obviously what counts!) I'm dismissing 1...h5 as it looks ridiculous. The two other options which can clearly be eliminated are:

1...♗g4 2 ♗xf7+ ♔xf7 3 ♘g5+ picking up the bishop and **1...♘d7? 2 ♗xf7+! ♔xf7 3 ♘g5+**

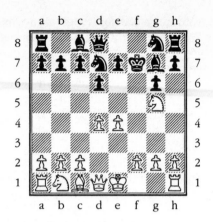

3...♔f6 (else 4 ♘e6) **4 ♕f3 mate**

Once you factor the above into the equation, only **A** provides a sound pairing. Incidentally the fact is that 1...♘f6 and 1...e6 are the most popular responses by strong Black players so the 5pts are well justified!

Q17

From our test position the game **Kavalek – Khodos**, Sinaia 1965 saw **1 ♖d8+!!**

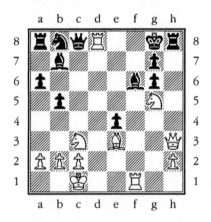

and then Black promptly resigned. Play might continue (briefly) with 1...♗xd8 (or 1...♕xd8 2 ♕e6+ ♔f8 3 ♕f7 mate) 2 ♕xh8+ ♔xh8 3 ♖f8 mate.

Suggestions B and D are dumb but I'm going to generously award 1pt to E. There is no point in dabbling in a tactic if you can't see it working and something less radical leaves you with a plus. Remember everyone loves to see show-offs fail!

Still it's 5pts for the delightful **C**.

Q18

Answer A makes no sense whatsoever. There is no reason why White should under-promote and as he retains a pawn on g3, he wouldn't be left with just two knights (and certainly not against a bare black king). The less said about all that the better and so moving swiftly on:

1...♚xa7 2 ♘c6+ ♚b7 3 ♘xb8 ♚xb8 4 ♚xc5 ♚c7 5 ♚b5 ♚b7 6 b4 (regaining the opposition) 6...♚c7 7 ♚a6 ♚b8 8 ♚b6 ♚a8 9 ♚c7 ♚a7 10 b5 ♚a8

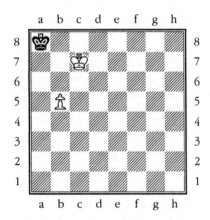

11 ♚b6 (Careful to avoid 11 b6 stalemate. Remember that provided it is not a rook's pawn, if the attacking king makes it to the 6th rank ahead of the pawn then he will win wherever the defender's king is and whoever is to move.) 11...♚b8.

1... ♚a6 ♚a8 13 b6 ♚b8 14 b7;

1...♝xa7 2 ♘c8+ ♚b7 3 ♘xa7 ♚xa7 4 ♚xc5 ♚b7 5 ♚b5 ♚a7 6 ♚c6 ♚b8 7 ♚b6 ♚c8 8 b4 ♚b8 9 b5 ♚a8 10 ♚c7 ♚a7 11 b6+.

In both cases the pawn marches to glory and so it's full marks to **E**.

103

Q19

The game **Kotov – Kholmov,** Moscow 1971, showed this position to be easy peasy lemon squeezy! Answers B-D may all have a tinge of logic to them but they don't come close to **1 🟥xc5! 🟥xc5 2 🟥c2 🟥fc8 3 ♛b5!**

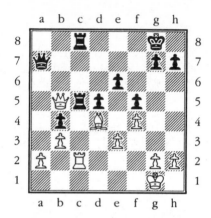

Yes, a theme that we've already seen in this very test (no excuses then if you didn't get it!). Black now resigned as both 3...🟥xb5 4 🟥xc8+ ♔f7 5 ♗xa7 and 3...🟥xc2 4 ♗xa7 would lose significant material. Anyway the 5pts go to **A**.

Q20

It should be clear to the reader that 1 🟥a7 intending 2 🟥xa6 won't be adequate as the king and pawn ending will be a draw. This is because the black king is near enough to prevent White's then passed a-pawn from promoting. However White can win by essentially employing this concept later. First though he must drive the enemy monarch sufficiently far away. It is a laborious task but one that nevertheless reaps a big reward (5pts for **A**):

1 🟥c7+

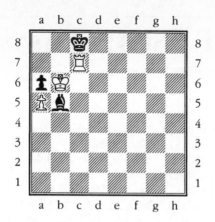

1...♚d8 (Although it may be tempting for Black to want to keep his king near the pawn, after 1...♚b8 2 ♜c2 there are serious mating issues. e.g. 2...♝f1 3 ♜f2 and 4 ♜f8 will be terminal.) **2 ♚b7 ♝e2 3 ♜c2 ♝b5 4 ♜d2+ ♚e7 5 ♚c7 ♚e6 6 ♜d4 ♝f1 7 ♜d6+ ♚e5 8 ♚c6 ♝e2 9 ♚c5 ♝b5 10 ♜b6 ♝d3 11 ♜b3 ♝f1 12 ♜e3+ ♚f4 13 ♚d4 ♝b5 14 ♜e5 ♝a4 15 ♜e6 ♝b5 16 ♜f6+ ♚g5 17 ♜f8 ♚g6 18 ♚c5 ♚g7 19 ♜a8 ♚f6 20 ♚b6 ♚e7 21 ♜xa6 ♝xa6 22 ♚xa6 ♚d7 23 ♚b7** and a promotion is inevitable.

I'm afraid that I can't really comment on E, which is of course too subjective.

Test Two: Answers

Q1

As seen in **Medina – Tal**, Mallorca, 1979 this should have been an easy 5pts to help you kickstart test two.

1...♕g1 2 ♕xd5 h2 3 ♕d8+ ♔h7 4 ♕h4+ ♔g8 5 ♕d8+ has allowed a perpetual check with 1...♕b1 2 ♕xd5 h2 3 ♗e1 worse still. I don't think that 1...♕h2+ changes much (other than missing the win!!) and 1...♕g2+ 2 ♕xg2 hxg2 3 ♔f2 ♘e3 (This knight can't be taken by the king but as you will soon see this move can be employed under far more beneficial circumstances.) 4 ♗b6 is certainly not advisable!

The continuation of **1...♕xf3+ 2 ♔xf3 ♘e3!**

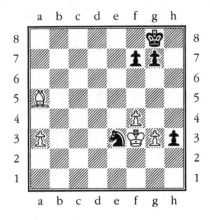

earning **B** the top marks, is decisive. The key idea is that the g2-square is guarded making ...h2-h1 unstoppable (even by the long range bishop).

Q2

I myself might have been tempted to select E (which by the way I am awarding 2 pts) were it not for the encounter (another recent one) **Bauer – Korchnoi**, France 2003 which saw **1 ♖g1+ ♔h8** and then the stunning **2 ♕d6!!**

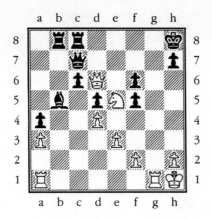

This beautiful deflection elicited a resignation. There is nothing that Black can do to prevent White's queen landing on f6 unless of course he wants to be humiliated by **2...♕xd6 3 ♘f7 mate!**

The maximum 5pts go to **C**.

Q3

1 ♕h5 is clearly no good in view of 1...♕e4+ 2 ♔a1 ♕g6 and the black queen defends. A relatively better try is 1 ♖g1 f6 2 ♖xb7+ (or 2 exf6+ ♔h6! and there is nothing doing.) 2...♔g6 but there doesn't seem to be anything convincing and a piece is a piece!

Coincidentally this position involved the same player as our last tactical puzzle only this time he was on the receiving end of **1 ♕f6+!!**

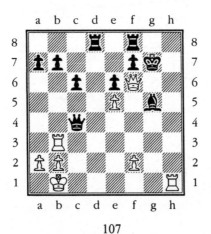

I do always say "look out for checks!" just in case there may be a good one you could do (or your opponent could do against you) and the one seen in **Apicella – Bauer**, France 2003 is pretty emphatic. Black resigned in view of 1...♝xf6 2 ♖g3+ ♝g5 3 ♖xg5 mate.

Obviously then I can't help but award 5pts for **E**.

Q4

It looks as though White is threatening to advance his rook to c6 in order to pick off Black's pawn but to draw this position Black must remain active. For example too passive is 1...♖g6 2 a5! bxa5 3 ♚a4 ♖g1 4 ♚xa5 ♖a1+ 5 ♚b6 ♚d6 6 ♚b7 ♖b1 7 b6 ♖a1 8 ♚b8 ♖a2 9 b7 ♚d7 (reaching the famous Lucena position) 10 ♖d3+ ♚e7 11 ♖d4

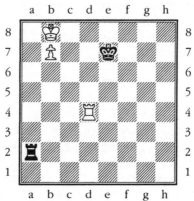

(building a bridge) 11...♖a1 12 ♚c7 ♖c1+ 13 ♚b6 ♖b1+ 14 ♚c6 and there is no satisfactory defence to ♖d5-b5.

Unfortunately A isn't of course applicable here and I'm afraid that I can't award anything for the generalisation of E (Where have I heard that one before?).

The maximum 5pts goes to **D** for 1...♖h4 2 ♖c6 ♖h3+ 3 ♚c2 ♖h2+ 4 ♚d3 ♖h3+ 5 ♚e2 ♖h2+ 6 ♚f3 ♖a2 7 ♖xb6 ♖xa4 and the remaining white pawn will soon drop e.g. 8 ♖b8 ♖b4 9 b6 ♚c6.

Q5

I really hope that you don't really feel like E (no pts!) as there is actually something to take from the position that we have actually picked up half way through a 1999 prize winning study of Kralin's.

Clearly there are stalemate issues to be considered e.g. the draw after 1 ♖xa7 h4 but White is actually winning:

1 ♖b7 h4 (White has time to take the pawn after 1...♔h4 i.e. 2 ♖xa7 ♔h3 3 ♖h7 h4 4 ♖xh4+ ♔xh4 5 a7 ♔g5 6 a8=♕ ♔f4 7 ♕d5 ♔g5 8 ♕xe5+ etc.) **2 ♖b6!!**

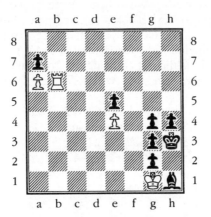

(The first key concept. White offers his rook to give himself a passed pawn and more critically give Black a move.)
2...axb6 3 a7 b5 4 a8=♘!! b4 5 ♘c7 b3 6 ♘e6 b2 7 ♘g5 mate.

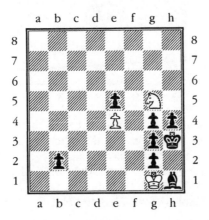

You won't call this unrealistic if you get this in a game! 5pts for the correct answer of **C**.

Don't you just hate it when you read phrases like "and White has excellent winning chances"! For crying out loud, does that mean White is winning or not? D of course then was a bit of tease. Sure centralising kings in endgames is generally a good idea and rooks do belong behind passed pawns. I guess there could even be an argument for 1 g4 to 'fix' Black's isolated pawn but the fact is that White must get to the crux of the matter here and now. If he loses his f-pawn (an inevitability) for Black's a-pawn then (despite some winning chances!) a theoretically drawn rook and three pawns vs rook and two pawns situation will have been reached. The only winning move is:

1 f8=♕+! (Drawn should be 1 ♔g2 ♔f8 2 ♖a7 ♖e7 3 ♖xa5 ♔xf7 and 1 ♖a7 a4 (or 1...♔f8 intending 2...♖e7) 2 ♔g2 (2 f8=♕+ ♔xf8 3 ♖xh7 ♖a5! 4 ♖c7 a3 5 ♖c1 a2 6 ♖a1 ♔g7) 2...a3 3 ♔f3 a2 4 ♖xa2 ♔xf7.) **1...♔xf8 2 ♖xh7 a4 3 ♖a7 ♖e4 4 ♔g2**

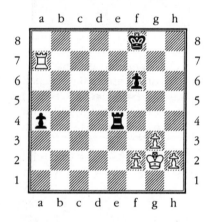

The important feature to note is that with the white rook behind the a-pawn it poses no danger. On the other hand, White can create serious threats with his two pawn majority on the kingside e.g. **4...♖b4 5 h3 ♔g8 6 g4 ♔f8 7 ♔g3 ♖b3+ 8 f3 ♖b4 9 h4 ♔g8 10 g5 fxg5 11 hxg5 ♖c4 12 f4 ♖b4 13 f5 ♖c4 14 f6 ♖b4 15 g6 ♖b8 16 ♔g4 ♖c8 17 ♔g5 ♖b8 18 ♔h6 ♖c8 19 f7+ 1-0**

You may feel that it was unlikely that a white pawn would be on f7 in this puzzle's starting position but in fact the only difference between this and Ward-Berry, 4NCL 2003 is that Black's pawn ~~were~~ *was* on f5 instead of f6. I went with 1 f8+ and won quickly so 5pts for **A**.

Q7

Wow this a pretty harsh question and I really hope I won't have offended in my opinion the greatest ever player but in **Huzman – Kasparov**, European Club Champs 2003 all I can say is that **1...♗c8??** was an absolute disaster. Indeed it was correctly punished by **2 ♖xd5!**

2...♕e8 (The rook was untouchable i.e. 2...♘xd5 3 ♕xg7 mate and 2...♕xd5 3 ♘e7+ ♔h8 4 ♘xd5 ♘xd5 5 ♕xc4.) **3 ♗xc4** when no doubt feeling as sick as a parrot Black threw in the towel.

I guess the other supplied options are sort of playable with observations being:

1...♖e8 as 2 ♗xc4? ♕c8! runs into hitting both f5 and c4;

1...♖c8 2 ♗xc4? ♗b8 and now it is the bishop on c4 that is pinned;

1...g6 2 ♘h6+ ♔g7 3 ♘g4 may feel unattractive but after 3...h5 4 ♘xf6 ♕xf6 Black retains his bishop pair advantage after all.

As there is no obvious refutation of the natural 1...♕d7, it has to be 5pts for **B**.

Everyone makes mistakes!

Q8

In **Harikrishna – Arkell**, Hastings Premier 2003 essentially a draw was agreed after **1 ♖g7+**.

However in the heat of the moment the English Grandmaster had obviously forgotten that the white queen was pinned and thus instead

of 1...♔h8 2 ♖g8+ ♔h7 3 ♖g7+ ♔h8 etc. he could have won via
1...♔h6! 2 ♖g8 (Rumour has it Keith kind of forgot that Black could
meet 2 ♖g6+ with 2...♕xg6.) **2...♗xg2+ 3 ♖1xg2 ♕xg8! 4 ♖xg8 e2
5 ♖e8 d3**

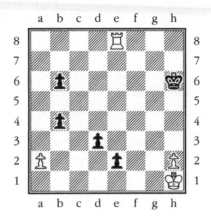

Above, the two passed pawns defeat the rook. 5pts for **E**.

Q9

Seen here in the French 'Fort Knox' variation but applicable in
other openings too, a very useful trap to take note of is:

1...♘f6 2 ♘xf6+ ♕xf6 3 ♗g5 ♗xf3 4 ♕d2!
and it's goodbye to the black queen (note 4...♕xd4 5 ♗b5+).

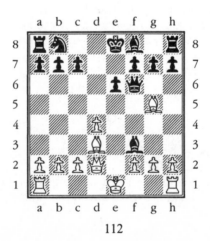

Equally sneaky after 1...♘d7 2 ♕e2 ♘gf6 3 ♘xf6+ ♕xf6 4 ♗g5 ♗xf3 is 5 ♕e3! again winning material.

Believe me I have come across people that subscribe to the point of view in E but despite any plugs I would like to make regarding my *Winning With The Dragon* books, I'm afraid that I can't condone that attitude!

5pts for **D**.

Q10

Apart from 1 ♘e7+ which just seems to give a piece away for nothing, all of the others seem quite reasonable. Earning **D** 5pts though, standing out in the crowd is the tactical continuation:

1 ♘d8!

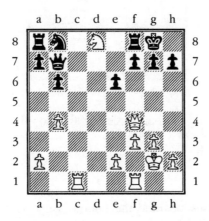

White targets f7 and that is seen in the most terminal of ways after 1...♖xd8 2 ♖c7. Upon 1...♕d5 2 ♖fd1 ♕f5 (or 2...♕xa2 3 ♕e4) 3 ♕xf5 exf5 4 ♖c8 Black's queenside would be paralysed but the **1...♕e7 2 ♕e4** of **Lipnitsky – Sokolsky**, Ukraine, 1949 was hardly much better.

White wins a significant amount of material and it is 5pts for **D**.

Q11

The triangulation theme isn't relevant here but some serious counting must be done if White is to squeeze out the black king. For example check out:

1 h4? ⹅f7! (Not 1...⹅h7? 2 h5! gxh5 3 ⹅xh5 and White gets the opposition.) 2 ⹅h6 ⹅f6 3 ⹅h7 ⹅f7 4 ⹅h8 ⹅f8 5 ⹅h7 ⹅f7 when White can make no progress.

On the other hand:

1 h3! ⹅**f7** (or 1...⹅h7 2 ⹅f6 ⹅h6 3 h4 ⹅h7 4 ⹅f7 ⹅h6 5 ⹅g8 ⹅h5 6 ⹅g7) **2** ⹅**h6** ⹅**f6 3 h4** ⹅**f7** (or 3...⹅f5 4 ⹅g7 ⹅xf4 5 ⹅xg6 and the h-pawn queens) **4** ⹅**h7** ⹅**f6 5** ⹅**g8**

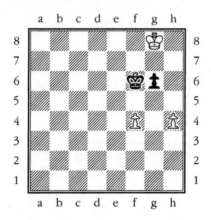

and the black king is soon forced to abandon the pawn: **5...**⹅**e6 6** ⹅**g7** ⹅**f5 7** ⹅**f7** ⹅**xf4 8** ⹅**xg6 1-0**

So it's 5pts for **B**.

Q12

From our starting position the famous game **Larsen – Spassky**, Belgrade 1970 saw **12...h4!**

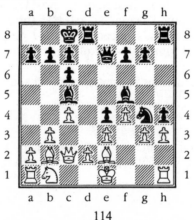

13 hxg4 (Similar to the game, 13 ♗xg4 ♗xg4 14 hxg4 hxg3 15 ♖g1 ♖h1! (15...♖h2 also looks extremely promising.) 16 ♖xh1 g2 17 ♖g1 ♕h4+ 18 ♔e2 (or 18 ♔d1 ♕f2) 18...♕xg4+ 19 ♔e1 ♕g3+ 20 ♔e2 ♕f3+ 21 ♔e1 ♗xe3 is pretty convincing too.) **13...hxg3 14 ♖g1 ♖h1! 15 ♖xh1 g2 16 ♖f1** (or 16 ♖g1 ♕h4+ 17 ♔d1 ♕h1) **16...♕h4+ 17 ♔d1 gxf1=♕+ 0-1** (The next up ...♗xg4+ will be terminal.)

For 5pts then **D** is pretty impressive although as there is clearly some compensation after 12...♘xe3 13 dxe3 ♗xe3 I'm going to award 2pts to B as well.

Unsound is 12...♖xd2 13 ♕xd2 ♗xe3 (Or 13...♘xe3 14 ♗a3! ♗xa3 (observe 14...♘g2+ 15 ♔f1 ♘e3+ 16 ♕xe3!) 15 ♘xa3 ♘g2+ 16 ♔f1.)14 ♕a5 when more material drops whilst 12...♗xe3 13 dxe3 ♘xe3 14 ♕c3 is too optimistic.

Being unprecedented in my generosity though I'm going to give another 2 pts for E.

If you don't believe that a sac works then unless it is for justifiable practical reasons (e.g. opponent's time trouble or sheer desperation!) you should refrain from employing it (particularly as here your position would be fine without it anyway).

Q13

Well, 1 ♘xd5 exd5 is hardly emphatic whilst 1 ♘db5 ♕c5+ and 1 ♗h6 ♘g6 both fail miserably. A joke is 1 ♘xe6 fxe6 and so the correct answer (5pts) is **C**:

1 ♘f5!

1...exf5 2 ♘xd5 and White will win material thanks to the threats against the black king and on the d-file. e.g. **2...♕c5+** (or **2...♕d8 3 ♘e3! ♕c7 4 ♖xd6 ♕xd6 5 ♗xe5**) **3 ♗e3 ♕xc2 4 ♘f6+ ♔h8 5 ♘xd7 1-0**

Sorry if I insulted your intelligence!

Q14

I have some sympathy for those that selected E but I'm afraid no points! Indeed it should be fairly obvious that Black to play mates via 1...♔b3+ and 2...♕b2 and so the big question surrounds the outcome were it White to move. It is a fairly amazing situation but even in the corner the black queen is a monster. It's 5 pts for **D** as Black is winning anyway:

1 ♔a2 ♕a8+ 2 ♔b1 ♕b7+ 3 ♔c1 ♕h1+;

1 ♕a4 ♕h1+ 2 ♔a2 ♕h2-b2 mate, and

1 ♕e3+ ♔c2+ 2 ♔a2 ♕b2 mate are fairly straightforward with the hardest to find win coming after **1 ♔b1 ♕h7+!!**

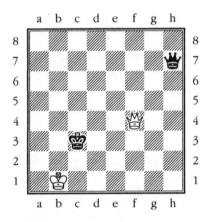

(The only winning move.) **2 ♔a1 ♕a7+ 3 ♔b1 ♕b6+ 4 ♔c1 ♕g1+ 0-1**

Q15

In **Bykhovsky – Oltean**, Berlin 1990 the sacrifice **1 ♗xh6! gxh6** was justified by the important **2 ♖d6!** (White has nothing after 2

♖g3+ ♔h8 or 2 ♕g6+ ♔h8 3 ♕xh6+ ♘h7 when in fact the piece is preferable to the pawns.)

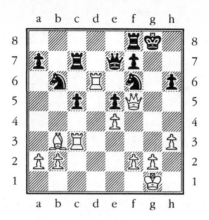

White hits the knight and **2...♘bd7** (The rook is out of bounds i.e. 2...♕xd6 3 ♕g6+ ♔h8 4 ♕xh6+ and Black can't interpose the knight as the queen would hang. On the other hand 4...♔g8 5 ♖g3+ isn't great either! Note upon 2...♘e8, 3 ♖xh6 mate is unavoidable.) **3 ♕g6+ ♔h8 4 ♕xh6+ ♘h7 5 ♖g3** and Black resigned in view of 5...♖g8 6 ♖xg8+ ♔xg8 7 ♖g6+ ♔h8 8 ♕g7mate.

So it's 5pts for **A** although I'm giving 2pts for those who selected E as with his bishop pair and pressure against the isolated c-pawn, White would have a clear advantage.

Q16

Well the connected pawns certainly are dangerous but they can be stopped. However not by:

1 ♘c4+ ♔e2 and the d-pawn rolls home; nor

1 ♘c6 c2! (Not 1...d2+? 2 ♔d1 with an easy blockade on c2.) 2 ♘b4 ♔e2 and with the d-pawn ready to move, 3 ♘xd3 ♔xd3 4 ♔b2 ♔d2 doesn't save the day; or even

1 ♔d1 c2+! 2 ♔c1 d2+! 3 ♔xc2 ♔e2 and the knight can't cover d1.

It is however 5pts for **B** as accuracy is required:

1 ♘b3 ♔e2 (upon 1...d2+ simplest is 2 ♘xd2 cxd2+ 3 ♔d1 ♔d3 stalemate!) **2 ♘d4+ ♔e1 3 ♘f3+ ♔f2 4 ♘e5 ♔e2**

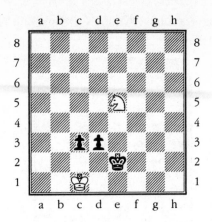

(Or 4...d2+ 5 ♔d1! ♔e3 6 ♘c4+ ♔d3 7 ♘xd2 – not forced but it does the job!) **5 ♘xd3!** (The only move!) **5...♔xd3 6 ♔d1 c2+ 7 ♔c1 ♔c3 ½-½**

Q17

How predictable was **E** (5pts!) and who better to supply that genius than the great man I was praising earlier (albeit as he was making an almighty howler!). Check out **Kasparov – Kramnik, Novgorod 1994.**

27 h5!!

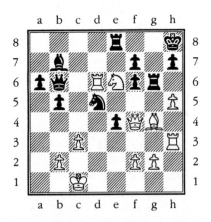

(You will soon see why this is clearly stronger than the murky 27 ♖xb6 ♘xf4 28 ♘xf4 ♖xg4.) **27...♘xf4** (Analysis by Grandmaster

118

Ftacnik concludes that each of 27...♕a5 28 hxg6 ♕a1+ 29 ♔c2 ♘b4+ 30 cxb4 ♖c8+ 31 ♘c5; 27...♖g7 28 ♕h6; 27...♖xg4 28 ♕xg4 ♖g8 29 ♕xg8+ ♔xg8 30 ♖xb6 ♘xb6 31 ♖g3+ ♔h8 32 ♘c5; 27...fxe6 28 hxg6 ♘xf4 29 ♖xh7+ ♔g8 30 ♖xb6; 27...♖xe6 28 hxg6 ♘xf4 29 ♖xh7+ ♔g8 30 gxf7+ ♔f8 31 ♖h8+ ♔xf7 32 ♗xe6+ ♘xe6 33 ♖xb6 are winning for Black whilst 27...♖gg8 28 ♖xd5! ♖xe6 29 ♗xe6 ♕xe6 30 ♖d6 is a clear advantage. There, don't say I never give enough variations!) **28 hxg6 ♕xd6** (or 28...♘d3+ 29 ♖hxd3! exd3 (The checks dry up after 29...♕a5 30 gxf7 ♕a1+ 31 ♔d2 ♕xb2+ 32 ♔e1 ♕c1+ 33 ♗d1) and each of 30 gxf7, 30 g7+ and 30 ♖xb6 would win.) **29 ♖xh7+ ♔g8 30 gxf7+ ♔xh7 31 fxe8=♕ ♘xe6 32 ♗f5+! ♔g7 33 ♕g6+ ♔f8 34 ♕xf6+ ♔e8 35 ♗xe6**

White is winning but in view of the 35...♗d7+ that would surely follow, **35...♕f8?** certainly accelerated things! **1-0**

Q18

In case you hadn't realised by now, you are unlikely to get far in these tests by answering questions with questions i.e. 0pts for E!

I for one can't see a win if it were a light-squared bishop instead as any positive winning attempt seems to result in stalemate. If on the other hand you do find a win (i.e. that doesn't involve Black making a sequence of poor 50-50 decisions!) then by all means contact the publishers and I'm sure(?!) they would be happy to refund your money! Regarding the original test position, let's try some moves:

1 ♗f6 ♔g8 (avoiding 1...gxf6?? 2 ♔xf6 ♔g8 3 g7 ♔h7 4 ♔f7) **2 ♗e5 ♔f8 3 ♔d7 ♔g8 4 ♔e7 ♔h8 5 ♗f6**

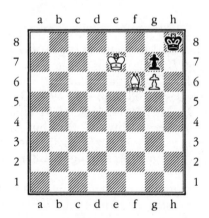

119

5...♔g8 6 ♔e6 (Not 6 ♔e8?? hoping for 6...♔h8 7 ♔f7 when Black must take the bishop and the g-pawn promotes because of the immediate 6...gxf6 and it's Black's newly passed pawn that would promote.) **6...♗f8! 7 ♔f5 ♔g8** (Again not 7...gxf6?? 8 ♔xf6 ♔g8 9 g7 ♔h7 10 ♔f7.) **8 ♗xg7 ♔xg7 9 ♔g5 ♔g8 10 ♔f6 ♔f8 11 g7+ ♔g8 12 ♔g6 ½-½**

The conclusion then is that despite being a piece up it is one of those rare situations in which one can't win. 5pts for **C**.

Q19

The famous game **Averbakh – Kotov**, Candidates Tournament 1953 looked so much fun:

33 ♔f5 ♘d7

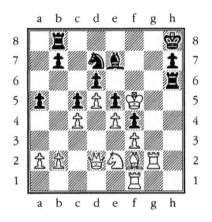

34 ♖g5 ♖f8+ 35 ♔g4 ♘f6+ 36 ♔f5 ♘g8+ 37 ♔g4 ♘f6+ 38 ♔f5 ♘xd5+ 39 ♔g4 ♘f6+ 40 ♔f5 ♘g8+ 41 ♔g4 ♘f6+ 42 ♔f5 ♘g8+ 43 ♔g4 ♗xg5! 44 ♔xg5 ♖f7 (threatening mate in two via ...♖g7+). **45 ♗h4 ♖g6+ 46 ♔h5 ♖fg7** (this time it's ...♖h6 mate that's threatened). **47 ♗g5 ♖xg5+ 48 ♔h4 ♘f6 49 ♘g3** (The only way to stop ...♖h5 mate.) **49...♖xg3 50 ♕xd6 ♖3g6 51 ♕b8+ ♖g8 0-1**

I am happy with the validity of that but also believe that 33...♘g4!! (preparing ...♖f8) 34 ♘xf4 ♖g8! (this time ...♖f6 is on the agenda) 35 ♘h5 ♖hg6! threatening ...♖f8 mating is a sound possibility.

Regarding other knight moves, the line 33...♘h5 34 ♖g5 ♖f8+ 35 ♔g4 ♗xg5 36 ♔h3 ♘g3+ 37 ♔g2 (not 37 ♔g4 ♖h4+ 38 ♔xg5 ♖h5+ 39 ♔g4 ♖g8 mate) 37...♖h2+! 38 ♔g1 ♖h1+ 39 ♔g2 is also interesting. I only said 'may be good too' and as maybe they are(!) I must award the maximum 5pts for **D**. As they are clearly winning though take 1pt a piece for B or C.

Q20

In view of the threat of ♖a8 mate the only under-promotion to consider would be 1...e1=♘+ but after 2 ♔d2 the rook would soon give itself up for the pawn leaving an easy draw (in case you didn't know, 2 knights vs a king is a draw unless at a critical moment the defender plays like a complete idiot!)

Preparing to block the check with **1...♘c1** looks promising but after **2 ♖xb2 e1=♕** (Not that it is a serious winning attempt, promoting to a rook simply allows 3 ♖b1+xc1.) **3 ♖b1+ ♔a2** White can draw by playing in a kamikaze manner i.e. **4 ♖a1+ ♔xa1**

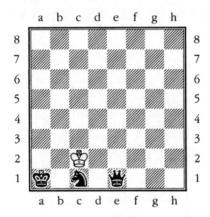

Stalemate! ½-½

A beautiful theme based on a study by **Vukcevich** means that **D** hits the 5pts jackpot! (Sorry E earns my sympathy but no points!).

Test Three: Answers

Defending this position looks like a pretty daunting task but the fact remains that it is possible (5 pts for **E**):

1...c2+ 2 ♔c1 ♔c3 (Or 2...a3 3 ♗xb4 a2 4 ♗c3! with stalemate helping out!) 3 ♗xb4+ ♔xb4 4 ♔xc2;

1...a3 2 ♗d6 ♔c4 (Or 2...c2+ 3 ♔c1 a2 4 ♗e5 when a suitable blockade would have been achieved.) 3 ♗f8 and there is nothing better than 3...♔b3;

As the main line then I have selected:

1...♔c4 2 ♗d6 b3 (Or 2...a3 3 ♗e7 ♔b3 4 ♗d6 a2+ 5 ♔a1 c2 6 ♗f4.) **3 ♗e7 ♔d3** (Observe 3...b2 4 ♗a3 ♔b3 5 ♗xb2!) **4 ♗d6 ♔d2 5 ♗a3! ♔d1 6 ♗c1 c2+ 7 ♔a1!**

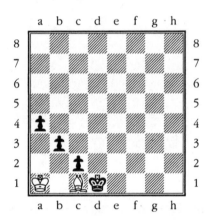

White has the dark squares covered and of course: **7...♔xc1** ½-½ (stalemate!)

Q2

Based on the recent game **Ye Jiangchuan – Xu Jun,** China 2003 by far and away the best continuation is **1 exf6!!** (Let's face it, it should have been an easy 5 pts for **B**!)

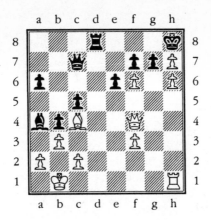

1...♜d1+ (The first idea to note is 1...♛xf4 2 hxg7 mate.) **2 ♜xd1** (2 ♚b2 would also win although now follows a most visual sequence.) **2...♛xf4 3 hxg7+ ♚xh7 4 ♜h1+ ♚g8 5 ♜h8 mate.**

Q3

I can tell you that the final part of **Ward – Devereaux**, 4NCL 2003 was extremely enjoyable to play. It seemed that it would be very difficult to win Black's f- and h-pawns but (with the king boxed in and the knight paralysed) my opponent was powerless to prevent the winning plan I had in mind:

1 ♚d5 ♝c3 2 ♚e6 ♝b2 3 ♚d7 ♝c3 4 ♚e8 ♝d2 5 ♝f7 ♝e3 6 ♝g6 ♝d2 7 ♝f8+ ♚h8 8 ♚f7 ♝xf4

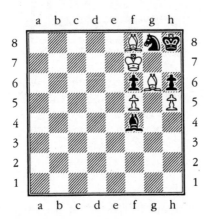

9 ♗g7 mate.

I'll give 2pts for A because that also crossed my mind. Nevertheless the top 5pts go to those who selected **C**.

Q4

After 1 ♖ea1 ♖xb2 2 ♕e1 (rather than 2 ♕xa5?? ♖b1+) 2...♘b4, there is no doubt that White would be on the back foot. 1 b3 and 1 ♖a2 are too passive and counterplay must be sought on the kingside. Unfortunately 1 ♘f6+? is unsound as 1...♘xf6! 2 exf6 ♖d4 picks up the d6-knight. Indeed as was discovered in the recent encounter **Avrukh – Rublevsky**, European Club Champs 2003 there is no need to be too clever as plenty of action comes with the most obvious attacking gesture:

1 ♖g3 ♔h8 (Black needed to prevent ♕xh6 but no better would be 1...♔h7 e.g. 2 ♕c2 ♔h8 3 ♘f6! gxf6 4 ♘xf7+! ♖xf7 5 ♕g6.) **2 ♘f6!**

2...♘f4 (After 2...♖xb2 the strength of White's onslaught is demonstrated in 3 ♘xf7+ (or 3 ♕xh6+ gxh6 4 ♘xf7+ ♖xf7 5 ♖g8 mate) 3...♖xf7 4 ♕xh6+ gxh6 5 ♖g8 mate.) **3 ♘d7 ♖d4 4 ♕xf4 ♖xf4 5 ♘xb6** White is a piece up and easily went on to win.

5 pts for **E**.

Q5

I feel pretty mean about this as all of the suggestions are quite good but I'm giving the 5 pts to the thematic choice of **D**:

Lalic – Zaja
Pula 1998

19 ♗f4!

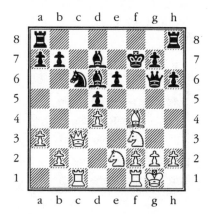

For me and obviously the strong Croatian Grandmaster too, this positional offering stands out from the others. It makes sense to eliminate Black's 'bishop pair' advantage. The text effectively forces the trade of bad for good bishop and in making more swaps, both the weak pawn on e6 and the outpost on e5 can be exploited.

19...♗xf4 (Black is unable to avoid the swap as after 19...♗e7 20 ♕b3! he can't deal with the dual threat of ♕xb7 and ♖xc6 (i.e. the fork on e5 is very much in the air).) **20 ♘xf4 ♕f6 21 ♘d3 ♖hd8 22 b4** (White has secured a good knight versus bad bishop scenario and the rest of the game is very smooth.) **22...a6 23 ♘c5 ♗c8 24 a4 ♔g8 25 b5 axb5 26 axb5 ♘a5 27 ♖a1 b6 28 ♘b3 ♗d7 29 ♘xa5 bxa5 30 ♖xa5 ♖ab8 31 ♕b4 ♖dc8 32 ♘e5 ♗e8 33 b6 ♕d8 34 ♖c5 ♖b7 35 ♖xc8 ♕xc8 36 ♕c5 ♕a8 37 h3 ♔h7 38 ♕c2+ ♔g8 39 ♖b1 ♕d8 40 ♕c5 ♕b8 41 ♖b3 ♕d8 42 ♘c6 ♗xc6 43 ♕xc6 ♕e7 44 ♖e3 ♔f7 45 ♖xe6 1-0**

Q6

You know I suppose it could go either way but I'm not going to award any points for E anyway because that's the sort of cruel heartless guy I am! Besides we're talking reality here and a more likely continuation is:

1 ♔g8 ♗c5 (1...♗h6 2 ♔h7 ♗f8 is of course merely a repetition.) **2 ♔f7 ♗d4 3 ♔e6 ♔b2 4 ♔d5 ♗g7** (A retreat of the king e.g. 4...♔c3 5 ♔d6 ♔c4 6 ♔c6 ♗h8 7 ♔b6 ♗g7 8 ♔c6 ♗d4 9 ♔d6 ♔c3 10 ♔d5 gets Black nowhere as he has to aim for White's a-pawn eventually anyway.) **5 ♔c4 ♔a3 6 ♔b5** (White is naturally hugging Black's b-pawn ready to take it as soon as the black king goes AWOL.) **6...♗f8 7 ♔a5**

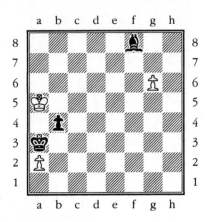

7...♔xa2 8 g7! (the necessary deflection) **8...♗xg7 9 ♔xb4 ½-½**

For 5pts clearly **D** is the most accurate solution. We all know that kings are extremely useful pieces in endgames but they aren't exactly long-range. Nevertheless it's quite amazing just how much distance the white monarch seemed to cover in order to salvage the draw.

Q7

Okay this was a bit of a crazy position but I saw a puzzle like this once and I'm afraid that I couldn't resist trying to reproduce something like the original. It's certainly a good test of your ability to analyse ahead although do note that even the likes of 'Fritz' doesn't get it for quite a while!

Anyway I wouldn't advise the optimistic 1 ♕xe6+?? ♖cxe6 2 ♕d8+ ♖d6 3 ♕a8+ ♖cc6 4 ♕a5+ ♔e6 which sees White running out of checks whilst 1 ♕b7?? ♖c1+ 2 ♔g2 ♖5c2+ 3 ♔f3 ♖e3 mate isn't too wise either. White can force a draw in a number of ways but the following continuation is quite beautiful:

1 ♕d8+ ♖d6 2 ♕b7+ ♖cc6 3 ♕a5+ ♖4c5 4 ♕b3+ ♖dc4

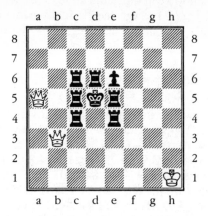

5 ♕d2+ ♖ed4 6 ♕f3+ ♖ee4 7 ♕g5+ e5 (Keep an eye on this pawn to observe the key to White's whole manoeuvring process. The point is that it won't be able to go backwards!) **8 ♕f7+ ♖e6 9 ♕d8+ ♖cd6 10 ♕b7+ ♖cc6 11 ♕a5+ ♖4c5 12 ♕b3+ ♖dc4 13 ♕d2+ ♖ed4 14 ♕f3+ e4 15 ♕g5+ ♖e5 16 ♕f7+ ♖de6 17 ♕d8+ ♖cd6 18 ♕b7+ ♖cc6 19 ♕a5+ ♖4c5 20 ♕b3+ ♖dc4 21 ♕d2 mate.**

I'm going to give 1 pt to A but it is the answer of **B** that gets the maximum 5pts.

Q8

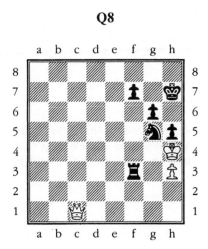

I have repeated the test position above to show why four of the five suggestions fail to keep the game alive:

Firstly 70...♖xh3+?? 71 ♔xg5 has basically just conceded a piece as there is certainly no mating net. Regarding the other 3, all of a sudden the concept of stalemate becomes a useful defensive weapon:

70...♘xh3 71 ♕h6+ ♔g8 72 ♕g7+ ♔xg7;

70...f6 71 ♕c7+ ♔h6 72 ♕h7+; and

70...♘e6 71 ♕h6+ ♔g8 72 ♕h8+.

Earning **A** 5pts because it keeps the game alive, the recent **Korchnoi – I.Sokolov**, European Club Champs 2003 saw **70...♖f5 71 ♔g3** ♘e4+ **72 ♔g2 h4 73 ♕c4 ♖f4 74 ♕d4 g5 75 ♕d3 ♔g6 76 ♔g1** ♔h6 **77 ♕d4 ♘f6 78 ♕c3 ♔g6 79 ♕c2+ ♖e4 80 ♔g2 ♔g7 81 ♕c3** ♖e6 **82 ♕d4 ♔g6 83 ♕d3+ ♘e4 84 ♕d8 ♘f6 85 ♕d3+ ♖e4 86** ♔g1 ♔g7 **87 ♕b5 ♔h6 88 ♕b7 ♔g6 89 ♕b1 ♔f5 90 ♕d3 ♔g6 91** ♕b1 g4 **92 hxg4 ♔g5 93 ♕c1+ ♖f4 94 ♕c5+ ♔xg4 95 ♕c7 ♘e4 96** ♕d7+ f5 **97 ♕g7+ ♘g5 98 ♕g8 h3 99 ♕g7 ♖e4 100 ♕c3 ♔h4 101** ♕f6 f4 **102 ♕d8 ♔g4 103 ♔f2 f3 104 ♕c8+ ♖e6 105 ♔g1 ♔f4 106** ♕f8+ ♔g3 **107 ♕b8+ ♔g4 108 ♕c8 ♔f5 109 ♕f8+ ♖f6 110 ♕c8+** ♔f4 **111 ♕c1+ ♔g4 112 ♔h2 f2 113 ♕f1 ♘f3+ 114 ♔h1 ♘d2** leading to the starting position for the next question!

Q9

I don't think that anything could be quite as amazing as A here which is of course why it is the wrong answer! What is remarkable though is that some 45 moves on from the last test position, again the game **Korchnoi – I.Sokolov**, European Club Champs 2003 witnessed a stalemate defence coming to the forefront.

After 115 ♕e2+ ♔h4 116 ♕f1 ♖f3! it's all over whilst 115 ♕d1+ ♖f3 116 ♕a4+ ♔g3 and Black mating White is inevitable provided of course he meets the trick 117 ♕f4+ with 117...♔xf4.

Hence play continued:

115 ♕xh3+!

(The resident theme from now is that White is more than happy to give away his queen as it would leave him with no other moves to make. Black tries hard to find a way to avoid taking it but to no avail.)

115...♔f4 116 ♕h4+ ♔e5 117 ♕g5+ ♖f5 118 ♕e7+ ♔f4 119 ♕d6+ ♔f3 120 ♕d3+ ♔g4 121 ♕g3+ ♔h5 122 ♕h3+ ♔g6 123 ♕g3+ ♔f7 124 ♕c7+ ♔e6 125 ♕c6+ ♔e5 126 ♕c3+ ♔e6 127 ♕c6+ ♔f7 128 ♕d7+ ♔g6 129 ♕d6+ ♖f6 130 ♕g3+ ♔f7 131 ♕c7+ ♔e6 132 ♕b6+ ♔e5 133 ♕c5+ ♔e4 134 ♕e7+ ♔f5 135 ♕d7+ ♔e5 ½-½

The correct answer of **D** earns 5pts.

Q10

I know what you may be thinking; surely this book shouldn't have an opening bias. Well generally it doesn't, but I was intrigued to find out (which in fact barring feedback, obviously I won't!) who amongst you would have been suckered in by the combination 5 ♗xf7+? ♔xf7 6 ♘g5+. Though it would succeed if Black simply moved his king, in fact it fails because after 6...♕xg5! 7 ♗xg5 ♗xd1 8 ♔xd1 Black emerges a piece up.

Even worse would be 5 ♘xe5?? ♗xd1 (or 5...♘xe5 protecting the bishop whilst retaining the attack on the white queen) 6 ♗xf7+ ♔e7 7 ♗g5+ ♘f6 which leads to nothing like the famous Legal's mate and as Black has done little wrong, why should it?

I'm going to award 2 pts for 5 d5 although it looks a little odd to be blocking the c4-f7 diagonal. It's also true that Black can respond with 5...♘d4 because of the pin but I don't believe that justifies the unambitious 5 dxe5.

Played by strong players but not in our line-up are 5 ♗b5 (which in moving the bishop again feels a little odd) and 5 h3 (because 5...♗xf3 6 ♕xf3 leaves Black having to deal with ♕xf7). Of the

129

selection though it has to be 5pts for **C** with for completeness, a reference below:

Rotstein – Rossi
Halkida 2000

1 e4 e5 2 ♘f3 ♘c6 3 ♗c4 d6 4 d4 ♗g4 5 c3

5...♘f6 6 0-0 (Another possibility is 6 ♕b3 e.g. 6...♘a5 7 ♗xf7+ ♔e7 8 ♕a3 ♔xf7 9 ♕xa5 c6 10 ♘g5+ ♔g6 11 ♕xd8 ♖xd8 12 h3 ♗c8 13 dxe5 dxe5 14 ♗e3 h6 15 ♘f3 ♗d6 16 ♘bd2 ♗b8 17 0-0-0 ♗e6 18 ♔c2 ♔f7 19 ♘e1 ♖d7 20 ♘d3 ♖dd8 21 ♘c5 ♗c8 22 ♘c4 b6 23 ♘d3 ♔e6 24 f3 ♗a6 25 b3 ♗c7 26 ♗f2 ♘h5 27 ♖d2 g5 28 ♖hd1 ♗xc4 29 bxc4 ♘f4 30 ♗e3 ♘xd3 31 ♖xd3 ♖xd3 32 ♖xd3 ♖d8 33 ♖xd8 ♗xd8 34 h4 gxh4 35 ♗xh6 ♔f6 36 ♔d3 ♔g6 37 ♗e3 ♗c7 38 a4 a6 39 ♔e2 ♔f6 40 ♔f2 ♔g6 41 ♔g1 b5 42 cxb5 axb5 43 axb5 cxb5 44 ♗c5 ♗a5 45 ♗b4 ♗b6+ 46 ♔h2 ♗f2 47 ♗d6 ♗g3+ 48 ♔g1 ♔f6 49 ♔f1 ♔e6 50 ♗c5 ♗f4 51 ♔e2 ♗g5 52 ♔f2 ♗d2 53 ♗b4 ♗f4 54 ♔e2 ♗g5 55 ♗f8 ♔f7 56 ♗d6 ♔e6 57 ♗c7 ♗f6 58 ♔d3 ♗g5 59 ♔c2 ♗f4 60 ♗d8 ♗g3 61 ♔d2 ♔f7 62 ♔e2 ♔g6 63 ♗e7 ♔h5 64 ♔d3 ♔g6 65 ♔e2 ♔h5 66 ♗f6 ♔g6 67 ♗d8 ♔h5 68 ♔d3 ♗f4 69 c4 ♗g5 70 ♗c7 1-0 Penrose-Trevelyan, Chester 1979.) **6...exd4 7 cxd4 ♗e7 8 ♘c3 0-0 9 ♗e3 a6 10 ♖c1 ♕d7 11 ♗e2 ♖fe8 12 h3 ♗xf3 13 ♗xf3 ♗f8 14 ♕c2 ♖e7 15 ♖fd1 ♕e8 16 ♗g5 ♘b4 17 ♕b3 ♘c6 18 ♗xf6 gxf6 19 ♘d5 ♕b8 20 ♗g4 ♗g7 21 ♖xc6 1-0**

This was (or at least should have been) a nice straightforward puzzle. We can eliminate 1 ♖xc7? ♗xd5 losing material and 1 ♘xe7 ♖xe7 which simply swaps off (not a great idea when you are down so much). Frankly 1 ♘b4 doesn't really carry a threat but I have to give 2pts for the materialistic B. Nevertheless after 1 ♘xc7 ♖c8 2 ♘xe8 ♖xc1 3 ♗xc1 ♘xe8 things are far from clear as Black's connected passed queenside pawns could prove a handful.

As you will see below it is **A** that gets the maximum 5pts:

Christiansen – Nunn
Germany 1989

1 ♘xf7+!!

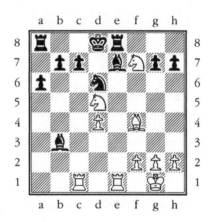

1-0 Yep that's it folks! Black resigned in view of **1...♘xf7** (Upon 1...♔d7 2 ♖xc7 is mate and White loses the house after 1...♔c8 2 ♗xd6 ♗xd5 (or 2...♗xd6 3 ♘b6+ ♔b8 4 ♖xe8+ ♔a7 5 ♖xa8+ ♔xb6 6 ♘xd6 cxd6 7 ♖b1) 3 ♖xc7+ ♔b8 4 ♖cxe7+ ♔a7 5 ♖xe8.) **2 ♗xc7+ ♔d7 3 ♘b6 mate**

This endgame seen in **Popovic – Bagirov**, Moscow 1989 is extremely instructive. White quite rightly rejected:

1 exf6 gxf6 2 gxf6 ♔f7 as White loses the f-pawn and he cannot then win because his remaining rook's pawn has an opposite coloured queening square to his bishop. Similarly 1 gxf6 gxf6 2 e6 ♔e7 3 ♔f2 b5 4 ♔e3 b4 5 ♔d4 f5 6 ♔c4 f4 7 ♔xb4 f3 8 ♔c3 f2 9 ♗a6 ♔xe6 has exactly the same flaw and that is why a more subtle approach was taken:

1 ♗f5!

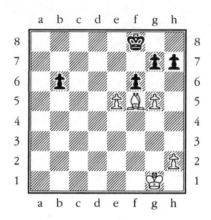

1...fxg5 (Upon 1...g6 White planned 2 ♗xg6! hxg6 3 gxf6 as after 3...b5 4 ♔f2 the white king is within 'the square' of the black b-pawn. Also with the bishop now blocking Black's f-pawn, 1...h6 2 gxf6 gxf6 3 e6! would be successful.) **2 ♗xh7 ♔f7 3 ♗f5 1-0**

5 pts then go to **C**.

Q13

In the recent encounter **Acs – Ivanchuk**, European Club Champs 2003, extremely accurate defence was required in order for Black to hold the draw. First of all note:

1...♔d4 2 ♔xf4 ♔d3 3 ♔g5 ♔e3 4 ♔xh5 ♔f2 5 g4;

1...♔d6 2 ♔xf4 ♔e6 3 ♔g5 ♔f7 4 ♔xh5 ♔g7 5 ♔g5 and White has the opposition;

1...f3 2 gxf3 ♔d4 3 ♔xh5 ♔e5 (or 3...♔e3 4 ♔g4) 4 ♔g5 and the white king escorts the pawn to promotion.

The correct answer for 5pts then was **D**:

1...h4! 2 ♔xf4 (Upon 2 ♔xh4 the black king returns in time to guard the f-pawn.)

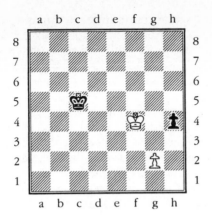

2...h3! (The only way to ensure that White couldn't take this pawn and then get the opposition too.) **3 gxh3 ½-½**

Yes here the players shook hands in view of **3...♔d6 4 ♔f5 ♔e7 5 ♔g6 ♔f8 6 ♔h7** (Or 6 h4 ♔g8 when as you should know the black king can't be budged from the corner.) **6...♔f7** with a standard draw.

Q14

Regarding the answer E, I think that's a little harsh as (even if you are a 1 e4 player) **Damiano's Defence** isn't exactly something you see every day. Also the little theory in existence on it is pretty much summarised below:

1 e4 e5 2 ♘f3 f6 3 ♘xe5 ♕e7

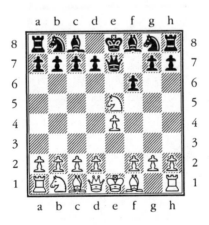

133

(With this Black sets a trap but anyhow it is forced in view of 3...fxe5? 4 ♕h5+ ♔e7 (or of course 4...g6 5 ♕xe5+ forking the king and rook) 5 ♕xe5+ ♔f7 6 ♗c4+ d5 7 ♗xd5+ ♔g6 8 h4 h5 (or 8...h6 9 h5+ ♔h7 10 ♗xb7! with 10...♗xb7 11 ♕f5+ in mind!) 9 ♗xb7 ♗xb7 10 ♕f5+ ♔h6 11 d4+ g5 when 12 ♗xg5+ nets the queen and 12 ♕f7 may be mate in 7 – just thought you'd like to know that!) 4 ♕h5+? (White has a nice inititiative after say 4 ♘f3 ♕xe4+ (or 4...d5 5 d3 dxe4 6 dxe4 ♕xe4+ 7 ♗e2) 5 ♗e2 as inevitable gain of tempi on the black queen leads to a big development advantage. Basically then the queen check is a big mistake and something that Black hopes for!) 4...g6 5 ♘xg6 (the h-pawn is pinned and White can meet 5...♕f7 with 6 ♘f4. However:) 5...♕xe4+ and the black queen takes the knight on g6 next turn.

As each of 3 ♘c3, 3 ♗c4 and 3 d4 make Black's opening play look silly the most accurate answer (for 5pts) must be **B**.

Q15

As White is in check I have little sympathy for those who selected E and what occurred in the recent encounter **Shumiakina – Sebag**, European Women's Club Champs 2003 was not too bright!:
    1 ♔g4??

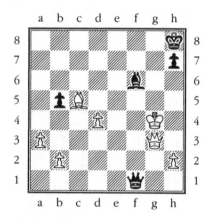

1...h5+! 2 ♔xh5 ♕f5+ 3 ♔h6 ♕h7 mate.

I believe that the correct answer is **A** (5pts) with the following justification:

134

1 ♕g2 ♕d3+ 2 ♔g4 (2 ♕g3 ♕f1+ is a straightforward repetition.) 2...♕g6+ 3 ♔f3 ♕f5+ 4 ♔g3 (or 4 ♔e2 ♕c2+ 5 ♔f1 ♕b1+) 4...♕g6+ 5 ♔f3 (White doesn't want to let the bishop into play the way 5 ♔f2 ♗h4+ 6 ♔f1 ♕b1+ does.) 5...♕f5+ (Not 5...♕d3+? 6 ♔f4 which leaves Black devoid of useful checks and White ready to regain the initiative.) 6 ♔g3 ♕g6+ and Black will achieve the desired perpetual check.

Q16

Come on guys surely this was money for nothing. Okay I'm going to award 2pts for those that selected E because 1 a4 is a pretty lame move. Indeed arguably Black starts to develop a bit of an initiative after 1...♕h4.

Fortunately I didn't give you an option of "Well I'd never get into this position in the first place!" because no doubt there would have been one or two takers! The point is that despite the fact that it's hardly a fantastic situation to deal with, that's your task nonetheless. More relevant I'm afraid is that I was consumed by a desire to include a 'Greek Gift' and hence 5pts go to **C**. White is not advised to continue as in the game **Swicarz – Jaracz**, Poland 2003:

1 ♘e2? ♗xh2+! 2 ♔xh2 ♕h4+ 3 ♔g1 ♘g4

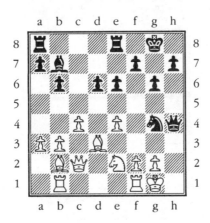

4 ♖fc1 ♕xf2+ 5 ♔h1 ♘e3 0-1

In view of the mate threat on g2 Black wins the white queen. I do always say 'look out for checks' and after 1 ♘e2? Evidently one of the two available to Black is a very strong one. No excuses then!

Q17

Three of the options can be eliminated:

1 ♗c6+? doesn't pick up the queen for nothing because of course 1...♘xc6 leaves it protected. Meanwhile 1 ♘f3? ♕xe4 simply doesn't work as Black's rook guards d8 and 1 ♘f5? (Evidently not a move that always works in Open Sicilians!) 1...♕xe4 flatters to deceive.

I'm going to award 1pt for **B** as 1 ♗xb7 ♕xe2 (Well done for calculating 1...♕xg5+? 2 f4 ♕xf4+ 3 ♔b1 ♘xb7 4 ♘xe6! fxe6 5 ♕xe6+ ♗e7 6 ♖hf1 forcing Black to concede his queen in order to avoid being mated.) 2 ♘xe2 ♘xb7 is fairly equal and better than everything except:

Cerquitella – Tomescu
Italy 2003

1 ♘xe6!! ♕xe6 (Unlike 1 ♗c6+? ♘xc6, this time 1...fxe6 2 ♗g6+! would win the black queen.) 2 ♗f5!!

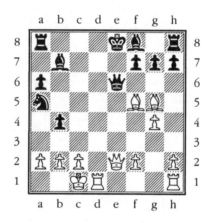

(With the black king caught in the middle other moves may work too but this is the most emphatic.) 2...♗e7 (The bishop pair combines particularly well on this open board after 2...♕xe2 3 ♗d7 mate.) 3 ♗xe6 ♗xg5+ 4 ♔b1 0-0 5 ♗d5 (Now White is a queen for two pieces up and the rest is plain sailing.) 5...♘c6 6 f4 ♗h4 7 g5 ♖ad8 8 ♕g2 ♖xd5 9 ♕xd5 ♘d8 10 ♕xd8 ♗xh1 11 ♕e7 1-0

It's 5pts for the correct answer of **D**.

Although lower rated players often rave about pawns in endings (after all they can turn into queens!), one can't underestimate minor pieces in endgames (especially bishops). If White is careful he can win but he must avoid saddling himself with the 'wrong rook's pawn'. Yes if his g-pawn becomes an h-pawn then it is a theoretical draw as White's light-squared bishop can have no control over the h8-square.

Three attempts fail:

1 ♔xe4 h3 and White can't preserve the pawn through 2 g3?? or else Black's h-pawn promotes;

1 ♔e3 h3 2 g3?? h2 is the same as above as this time the pawn on e4 obstructs the critical diagonal (thus stopping the bishop from halting the errant h-pawn);

1 ♗xg4 ♔g5 2 ♗d7 h3!! 3 ♗xh3 ♔f4 when both 4 ♔c3 ♔g3 5 ♔d4 (upon 5 ♔d2 ♔f2 White must relinquish his g-pawn in order to halt the black passed pawn.) 5...♔f4 and 4 ♗d7 ♔g3 5 ♗h3 ♔f4 will merely result in repetitions.

The correct technique (being **C** for 5pts) is illustrated below:

1 ♗c6!

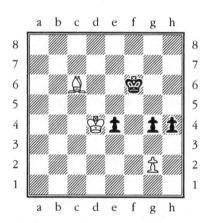

1...♔f5 (If 1...g3 then White should prevent his g-pawn from becoming an h-pawn via 2 ♗d7! Following this Black's pawns will fall easily.) **2 ♔e3!** (It is essential that the black king is kept out of the serious action.) **2...g3** (Upon 2...♔e5 all of Black's pawns drop quickly e.g. 3 ♗xe4 ♔f6 4 ♔f4 h3 5 g3 h2 6 ♔xg4 ♔e5 7 ♗h1 ♔f6 8 ♔h3) **3 ♗b7!** (A dinky waiting move. Absolutely vital was that White avoided 3 ♗xe4+? as provided Black avoided 3...♔g4?? (i.e. he should move to a dark square) 4 ♗b7 he would be able to play...h3 next. Note 3 ♗d7+! ♔e5 4 ♗c8 ♔d5 5 ♔f4 would of course transpose.) **3...♔e5** (or 3...♔g5 4 ♗c8!) **4 ♗c8 ♔d5 5 ♔f4 ♔d4 6 ♔g4 e3 7 ♗a6 ♔e4 8 ♔xh4 ♔f4 9 ♗e2** and a second decisive pawn must drop. **1-0**

Q19

Answer A couldn't be more incorrect. First of all as it is White to play, it is Black who officially has 'the opposition'. Secondly as his king isn't ahead of the b-pawn he wouldn't be able to win anyway. A reasonable general rule is that 'when you are up you should trade off pieces, not pawns and conversely when you are down you should trade off pawns not pieces'. Needless to say then it will very rarely favour the attacker to have a pair of pawns eliminated in such a manner as A suggests.

The problem from White's point of view is that his b-pawn is one square too far forward or his h-pawn is too far back. No amount of futile triangulation is going to aid this situation:

1 ♔d3 (Also justifying the correct answer of **E** we have 1 b4+ ♔b5 2 ♔b3 ♔b6 3 ♔c4 ♔c6 4 b5+ ♔b6 5 ♔b4 ♔b7 6 ♔c5 ♔c7 7 b6+ ♔b7 8 ♔b5 ♔b8 9 ♔c6 ♔c8 10 ♔d6 (or 10 b7+ ♔b8 11 ♔b6 stalemate.) 10...♔b7 11 ♔e6 ♔xb6 1... ♔f5 ♔c6 13 ♔g5 ♔d6 14 ♔xh4 ♔e6 15 ♔g5 ♔f7) **1...♔b4 2 ♔e3 ♔xb3 3 ♔f4 ♔c4 4 ♔g4**

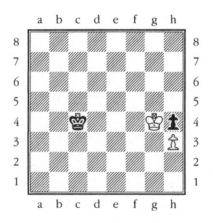

4...♔d5 5 ♔xh4 ♔e6 6 ♔g5 ♔f7 and the black king has made it back in time to the relevant corner. ½-½

Q20

It should go without saying that in **Ward – Matthiesen**, Copenhagen Open 2003 I was more than happy with the game continuation of **1 ♕xa7! ♗c5** (Upon 1...♗b8 the white queen can park itself on either a5 or a8. It remains a real nuisance and is in no serious danger.) **2 ♕a8+!** (My opponent was hoping to embarrass this queen but he was in for a bit of a shock!) **2...♔c7** (After 2...♔d7 3 ♕xb7+ ♔e8 4 ♕xc6+ Black is four pawns down with a lousy king!)

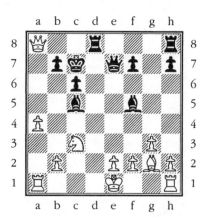

3 ♘b5+! cxb5 4 ♕xb7+ ♔d6 5 ♕c6+ ♔e5 6 f4+ 1-0 (Mate would follow shortly.)

The other four suggestions were far from ridiculous but I'm afraid there is no reward for them as **E** takes the full 5pts.

Test Four: Answers

Q1

The correct answer for 5pts is **E** because the black king can force the white a-pawn to the 7th rank:

1 ♘c8 (Checking out the other alternatives we have 1 ♘b5 ♚c6 2 ♔g2 ♚b6 3 a7 ♚b7 and 1 ♔g2 ♚c5 2 ♘c8 ♚c6 3 ♔f3 (or 3 ♘d6 ♚b6! but it wasn't that difficult to spot!) 3...♚c7 4 a7. It just isn't possible for White to protect the pawn on the 6th rank.) **1...♚c6 2 ♔g2 ♚c7 3 a7**

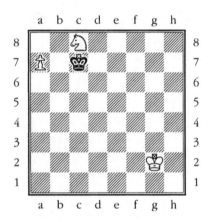

3...♚b7 4 ♔f3 ♚a8 5 ♔e4 ♚b7 6 ♔d5 ♚a8 7 ♚c5 ♚b7 8 ♚b5 ♚a8 and no progress can be made. ½-½

The win would be trivial if White could arrange say the pawn on a6 and the knight on b4. Then he could retrieve his king and convert at his own leisure. With the pawn on a7 though and the black king nestled in the corner the white monarch can't come too near for fear of stalemate.

Q2

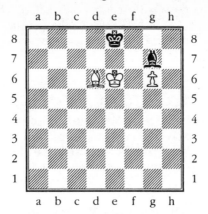

From the test position repeated above, the first thing to note (with White to play) is that 1 ♗e5 doesn't win because of 1...♔f8! (i.e. rather than the immediate trade 1...♗xe5?? which is lost after 2 ♔xe5 ♔e7 3 ♔f5 ♔e8 4 ♔e6! ♔f8 5 ♔f6 ♔g8 6 g7 ♔h7 7 ♔f7) when the king and pawn versus king ending is drawn after 2 ♗xg7+ ♔xg7 3 ♔f5 i.e. 3...♔g8 4 ♔f6 ♔f8 5 g7+ ♔g8 6 ♔g6.

Of course White is not obliged to employ 1 ♗e5 but the key thing for Black to remember is that he should return his bishop to g7 as soon as that threat becomes a reality e.g. 1 ♗a3 ♗c3 2 ♗c5 ♗b2 3 ♗d6 ♗g7!. Essentially then he is seeking to avoid the scenario that he would find himself in if he were on the move in our starting position. Yes in that instance he is lost with one possible continuation being: **1...♗h6** (Both 1...♗f8 2 ♗xf8 and 1...♗c3 2 ♗e5 are easy White wins.) **2 ♔f6 ♗d2 3 ♔g7! ♗c3+ 4 ♔h7 ♗d4 5 ♗f4**

(White is preparing to squeeze Black's bishop off of the vital a1-h8 diagonal and there is little that Black can do about it.) **5...♗c3 6 ♗h6 ♗d4 7 ♗g7 ♗c5 8 ♗c3 ♗f8 9 ♗b4** (a cruel final deflection that can't be ignored!) **9...♗xb4 10 g7** and the pawn promotes.

5pts for **B**.

Q3

Oh dear, I guess I've dug myself into a bit of a hole regarding E and because of the way I phrased the question I suppose I'd better award it 3pts. This book is only supposed to be a bit of fun though and so the full 5pts go to **A**, justified by the following recent encounter:

Yu Shaoteng – Wu Wenjin
China 2003

1...♘g3+!! 2 hxg3 hxg3

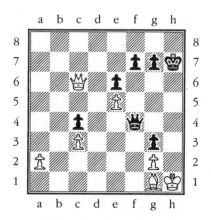

(Now 3...♛h4 and 3...♛h6 threatened to terminate the proceedings.) **3 ♗d4** (Or 3 ♗h2 ♛c1+! (rather than 3...♛h4 4 ♔g1 allowing White to stay alive) 4 ♗g1 ♛h6+ 5 ♗h2 ♛xh2 mate.) **3...♛h6+** (Similarly 3...♛c1+ 4 ♗g1 ♛h6+ 5 ♗h2 ♛xh2 mate.) **4 ♔g1 ♛c1 mate.**

Barring the technical debate regarding the rules of practical play, this wasn't exactly a tough question!

You were right if you had concluded that E was a load of twaddle! I have repeated the test position below again to help demonstrate the correct answer:

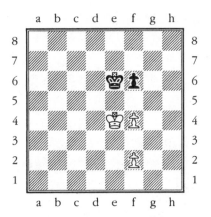

Firstly the truth is that with Black to play he loses:

1...♔d6 2 ♔f5 ♔e7 3 ♔g6 ♔e6 4 f5+ ♔e5 5 f3 ♔f4 6 ♔xf6 and the most advanced f-pawn will promote;

1...♔f7 2 ♔f5 ♔g7 3 ♔e6 ♔g6 4 f5+ ♔g5 5 f3;

1...♔e7 2 ♔d5 ♔d7 3 f5 ♔e7 4 ♔c6 ♔f7 5 ♔d7 ♔g7 6 ♔e7 and Black must give up the ghost.

I suppose that the toughest part of the question was trying to establish whether White would win if it was his turn. There appears to be two serious attempts:

1 ♔f3 f5! 2 ♔e3 ♔d5 3 ♔d3 ♔c5 4 ♔e3 ♔d5 5 ♔f3 ♔e6 (i.e. Black has accurately returned to square one where he is best prepared to prevent an invasion on either side.) 6 ♔g3 ♔f6 7 ♔h4 ♔g6 8 f3 ♔h6 and there is no way through;

1 f5+ ♔d6! 2 ♔f4 ♔d5 3 ♔g4 (or 3 ♔g3 ♔e5 4 ♔g4 ♔e4) **3...♔e4 4 f3+ ♔e5** (This is zugzwang. If Black were forced to move again then he would be lost but the reality is that it is White to play and so it's a draw.) **5 f4+ ♔e4** and it is a white pawn that drops. ½-½

For 5pts then the correct answer is **A**.

Q5

This puzzle based on standard endgame theory is intriguing (well I think so anyway!). The correct answer for 5pts is **C**, justified by the following analysis:

1 ♔g4 (1 ♔e4 ♔e6 2 f4? f6 3 f5+ is a draw as explained in the answer to the previous question.) **1...♔g6 2 f4 f6**

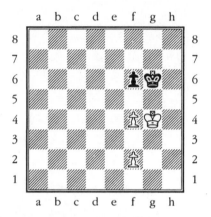

3 f5+ ♔f7 4 ♔h5 ♔g7 (Obviously necessary to prevent the decisive penetration.) **5 f3! ♔h7 6 ♔g4 ♔g7** (or 6...♔h6 7 ♔f4 ♔h5 8 ♔e3! ♔g5 9 ♔e4 ♔h5 10 ♔d5 ♔h6 11 ♔e6 ♔g5 12 f4+ ♔xf4 13 ♔xf6) **7 ♔f4 ♔f7 8 ♔e4 ♔e7 9 ♔d5 ♔d7 10 f4** (Proving that the second f-pawn was vital as the move has transferred to Black. He must give way and the rest is basic stuff.) **10...♔e7 11 ♔c6** (This is the reason why first feigning to go to the kingside and then returning (rather than vice versa) works. There is more room to penetrate i.e. here there is a c-file but the other way around there is no 'i' file!) **11...♔f7 12 ♔d7 ♔f8 13 ♔e6 ♔g7 14 ♔e7 ♔g8 15 ♔xf6 ♔f8 16 ♔g6 ♔g8 17 f6 ♔f8 18 f7 ♔e7 19 ♔g7 1-0**

Q6

I suppose 1...exf4 is okay and I'm going to award 1pt for the adventurous 1...♘xe4 2 ♘xe4 ♖xc2 3 ♕xb4 ♖xe2 because there is some compensation. Nothing though for 1...♗xe4 2 ♘xe4 ♖xc2 3 ♕xb4 ♖xe2 4 ♘xf6+ ♗xf6 nor 1...d5 2 fxe5 ♘xe4 3 ♘xe4 ♖xc2 (3...dxe4?? 4 ♕xd7) 4 ♕d1! which both seem to fail.

Clearly for 5pts the best answer is **C**:

Stripunsky – Goldin
Philadelphia 1999

1...♖xc3! 2 ♕xc3 ♘xe4

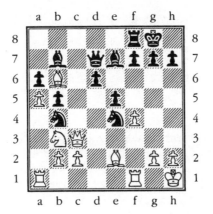

and White resigned in view of **3 ♕xb4** (Anywhere else leads to a significant material loss). **3...♘g3+! 4 hxg3 ♕h3+ 5 ♔g1 ♕xg2 mate**

Q7

I'm going to award 2pts for D particularly in view of 6...♘d4 7 ♘xe5? ♕e7 8 ♘d3?? ♘f3 mate!

Hardly inspirational are 6...♘e7 and 6...♘b8 but 6...e4?? definitely turns out badly:

Petrosian – Ree
Wijk aan Zee 1971

7 dxc6 exf3

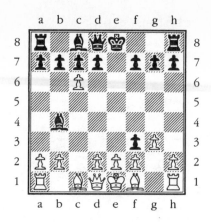

8 ♕b3! 1-0

Presumably Black had spotted 8 cxb7 ♗xb7 9 ♕b3 fxe2 when the
h1-rook is attacked, but missed this. If the bishop moves now or
after say 8...♕e7 9 a3, then the pawn fork on b7 wins significant
material. Hence Black (a Grandmaster no less!) resigned earning **B**
the 5pts.

Q8

This test position comes from a possible variation from the very
recent encounter **G.Flear – Illescas Cordoba**, European Champs
2003

Let's check out a couple of possible lines:
1 f3 ♕xa2 2 ♖xa2 d2 3 ♖xd2 (Or 3 ♖a1 ♘f2+ 4 ♔g1 d1=♕+ 5
♖xd1 ♘xd1 6 a5 ♘c3 7 b6 axb6 8 axb6 ♘e2+ 9 ♔f2 ♘d4 10 ♔e3
♘c6 and the knight has made it back.) 3...♘xd2 4 a5 ♘c4 5 b6 and I
suppose 5...♘xb6 6 axb6 axb6 is simplest (Black wins);
1 ♕b2 (or 1 ♕a1 d2 2 ♕d4) 1...d2 2 ♕d4 ♕f3 3 ♕d8+ ♔f7 4
♕d7+ ♔f6 5 ♕d4+ ♔e6 6 ♕c4+ ♔e5 7 ♕c7+ ♔d4 8 ♕d8+ ♔c3 9
♕c7+ ♔b3 and White has run out of checks.

Despite the above I believe that the computer was unable to
analyse far enough ahead. The main line should be:
1 ♕xf7+ ♔xf7 2 a5 d2 (If 2...♔e6 then 3 b6 axb6 4 a6 and there is
no stopping the a-pawn.) 3 ♖g1 ♘xf2+ 4 ♔g2 d1=♕ 5 ♖xd1 ♘xd1
6 b6

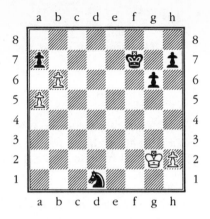

6...axb6 7 axb6! (Rather than 7 a6?? ♘e3+ 8 ♔f3 ♘d5 and the knight will defend all on c7.)

The conclusion for 5pts must be **D**.

Q9

I thought I'd give your brain a bit of a rest after the last puzzle and hopefully you noticed that the pawn on h3 was attacking the bishop!

Anyway I wouldn't be too enamoured by 1...♗d7 2 d4 ♗c6 3 ♘c3 ♘d7 4 e4 as Black would be over-run in the centre. I will award 2pts for C (1...♗f5) although I still have those concerns. Safest is 1...♗xf3 (**E** gets 5pts) as it at least allows Black to develop quicker. Plus there is that good old bit of advice about trading pieces when you are cramped. Whatever you do you should avoid:

Schmitt – Pribyl
Altensteig 1990

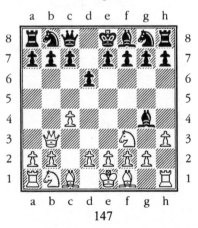

4...♗h5?? 5 ♕b5+ 1-0

Relax though, I'm not deducting any points for those that didn't look out for checks!

Q10

Answer A is of course complete rubbish whilst Black is hardly going to fit in with plan B! It seems harsh (as those pawns may have been stuck there ages ago) but I have to give the 5pts to **E** with the justification below:

1 ♔g2 (White is unable to activate his king via 1 ♔e1 ♔e3 2 g5 ♗e8 3 ♗c2 (Well, in view of the next up 3...♔f4, there are no serious winning attempts.) 3...♔xf3 and no different is 1 ♗e2 ♗a4 2 ♔e1 (or 2 ♔g2 ♗b3 3 ♔h3 ♗a4 4 ♔h4 ♗e8.) 2...♔e3 3 g5 ♗e8) **1...♗c4 2 ♔h3 ♗b5 3 ♔h4 ♗e8 4 g5 ♗g6**

(Black must prevent the white king from advancing but it is an easy task.) **5 ♗e2 ♗e8 6 ♗d3 ♔xf3 7 g6 ♗xg6 ½-½**

The blockade is a good one.

Q11

I suppose 1 ♗b3 is sensible and after 1 ♘xe6 fxe6 2 ♗xe6, as the e6-bishop is a bit of a pain, there must be some compensation (1pt then for the ambitious A). Both C and E are rubbish though and hence the following game rubber stamps my decision to give 5pts for **B**:

Ernst – Gruvaeus
Sweden 2000

1 ♗xe6! fxe6 2 ♘xe6 ♕b6 (2...♕a5 3 b4! with ♘d5 to follow wouldn't be much different.) **3 ♘d5! ♘xd5** (Probably Black should plump for the not great 3...♕c6 4 ♘ec7+ ♔f7 5 ♘xa8.) **4 ♕xd5 ♕b7**

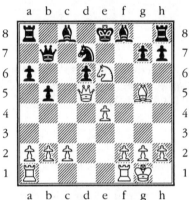

(Observe 4...♗b7 5 ♘c7+! ♕xc7 6 ♕e6+ mating.) **5 ♘xg7+ 1-0** Actually 5 ♘c7+ would have been even quicker but anyway Black resigned now in view of: **5...♗xg7 6 ♕e6+ ♔f8 7 ♗e7+ ♔e8 8 ♗xd6+ ♔d8 9 ♕e7 mate.**

Q12

Regarding A, there is a time and a place for everything and this isn't it! There is however a strong sacrifice available although the move order must be right:

Rublevsky – D'Amore
Mens Olympiad 2000

1 ♗xg5! (Upon 1 ♗xf7+ ♔xf7 2 ♗xg5 there is no compulsion for Black to take this second bishop as he already has a piece in the bag. Meanwhile 2 ♘xg5+ hxg5 for what it's worth, leaves the black rook guarding h5.) **1...hxg5 2 ♗xf7+! ♔xf7** (Instead 2...♔f8 3 ♗d5 ♖b8 4 ♘xg5 is horrendous.) **3 ♘xg5+**

149

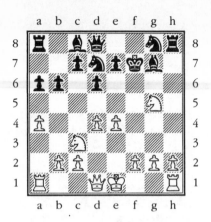

3...♔f6 4 ♕g4 (Threatening amongst other things 5 ♕f5 mate.)
4...♘e5 5 ♘d5+ ♔g6 6 ♘f4+ ♔f6 7 dxe5+ dxe5 8 ♘h7+ 1-0 (As it's mate next turn with 9 ♕g6, the 5pts go to **C**.)

Q13

The finish to the following game is pretty stunning:

Alfred – Marzolo
European Club Champs 2000

1...♘xa2+ 2 ♘xa2 ♕xa2

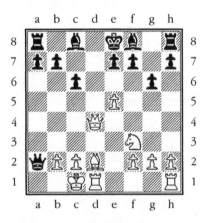

3 ♕d8+!! ♔xd8 4 ♗a5+ ♔e8 5 ♖d8 mate.

As 1...♛xa2 simply blunders a queen, by a process of elimination the variation 1...c5 2 ♛c4 ♝e6 3 ♛b5+ ♛xb5 4 ♞xb5 ♞a6 earns **E** the maximum 5pts.

Q14

After 1 ♛e2 0-0-0 2 ♞xe6 ♜e8, instead of 2...fxe6 3 ♛xe6 (which is only an equal ending that White could get via 1 ♛g4), Black has 3...♜e8 leaving him a pawn up.

Instead 1 ♞xe6 fxe6 2 ♛h5+ ♚d8 looks promising for White and better still:

1 ♞xf7!!

1...♚xf7 (Or 1...♛xf7 2 ♝xd5 as the bishop is pinned to the king.) **2 ♛f3+ ♚g8** (Also curtains is 2...♚g6 3 ♜xe6+! ♛xe6 4 ♝d3+ with 2...♚e8 3 ♝xd5 far from appetising!) **3 ♜xe6! ♛xe6 4 ♝xd5** (Or the cute 4 ♛xd5 ♛xd5 5 ♝xd5 mate.) **1-0**

There can be no doubt that **D** earns all 5pts.

Q15

To be honest, all of the options look feasible but as demonstrated by a promising English junior, it is **D** (5pts) that packs a real punch:

Kwiatkowski – Rendle
Hastings Challengers 2000

1...♛c7! (An extremely powerful quiet move. Black simply prepares 2...♘b6 3 ♛b5 ♗d7 with extreme embarrassment to the white queen.) **2 ♘f1?**

Not the best, but White experiences difficulties whatever:

2 ♗b1 b5! 3 ♛xb5 ♗a6 4 ♛a4 ♘b6 winning the queen;

2 ♗f1 ♘b6 3 ♛b5 a4 (or 3...♗d7!?) 4 ♘c5 ♖a5 5 ♛d3 ♗xc5 6 dxc5 ♘d7 dropping a pawn;

2 ♗e2 ♘b6 3 ♛b5 a4 (or 3...♗d7!?) 4 ♘c5 ♖a5 5 ♛d3 ♗xc5 6 dxc5 ♘d7 7 ♗xg4 ♘dxe5 8 ♛h3 ♖xc5 and again Black is a pawn to the good with positional extras to boot.

2...♘b6 3 ♛b5 a4

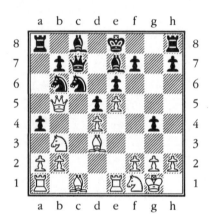

0-1

Oops! Having his offside queen position exploited, White now loses a piece as moving the knight allows 4...♖a5.

Q16

I have sympathy for E because Black's opening hasn't exactly been a success. White has obtained an attractive pawn centre but taking one now is not the solution:

1...♛xd4 2 ♛a4+! (Cute is that 2 ♗d2 ♛f6! keeps the pawn pinned as does 2 ♗b2 ♗a5!) **2...♘c6**

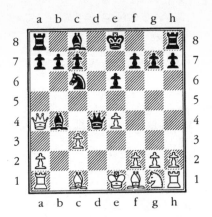

3 ♕xb4! ♘xb4 4 cxd4 ♘c2+ 5 ♔d2 ♘xa1 6 ♗b2

White will pick up the knight and as the two pieces are superior to the rook and pawn, he has a clear advantage. 5pts for **A**.

Q17

An easy bit of counting should eliminate 1 ♔c5 ♔xh4 2 ♔b5 ♔g4 3 ♔xa5 h4 4 ♔b6 h3 5 a5 h2 6 a6 h1=♕.White is miles off the pace. Instead the game **Khenkin – Ward**, French League 2002 saw:

1 ♔e5 ♔g4!

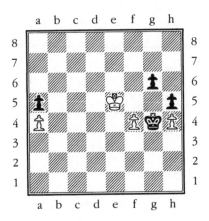

153

(Far superior to 1...♚xh4 2 ♚f6 ♚g4 3 ♚xg6 ♚xf4 (Or admittedly 3...h4 4 f5 h3 5 f6 h2 6 f7 h1=♕ 7 f8=♕ which should surely be a draw.) 4 ♚xh5 ♚e4 5 ♚g4 ♚d4 6 ♚f4 ♚c4 7 ♚e3 ♚b4 8 ♚d3 ♚xa4 9 ♚c2 ♚a3 10 ♚b1 when the white monarch has worked hard to achieve a result.)

0-1 in view of 2 ♚f6 ♚xf4 3 ♚xg6 ♚g4 4 ♚f6 ♚xh4 5 ♚e5 ♚g3 and the h-pawn queens.

I'm going to give 1pt to D but it is **E** that deserves the full 5pts.

Q18

I suppose that it is a bit late in the day to start confusing you with logic but no doubt there is one reader who concluded that more than one answer will have been valid! Well in fact E isn't right either as there is nothing false about **D** (5pts):

Sambuev – Smirnov
Krasnoyarsk 2003

1 ♘g5!!

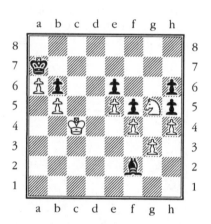

(After 1 ♘d4 ♝xd4 2 ♚xd4 there would be no way in for the white king. The test move is a corker!) **1...hxg5** (After 1...♝xg3 2 ♘xe6 ♝xh4 3 ♘d4 ♝g3 4 e6 ♝xf4 5 ♘xf5 ♝g5 6 ♚d3, Black will have to give his bishop up for the e-pawn making it a trivial win.) **2 hxg5 ♝c5** (The bishop must hurry to keep tabs on the passed g-pawn.) **3 ♚d3 ♝e7 4 ♚e2** (Black is powerless to prevent a simple invasion by the white king via the h-file.) **1-0**

154

Q19

All bar one of the candidate moves are reasonable and the drawback of that one is highlighted in the following recent game:

Izbinski – Miton
Poland 2003

1 ♗g5? ♛d5!

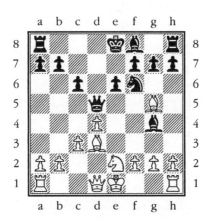

At every level (yes even Grandmasters!) one has to keep tabs on the undefended pieces. The pawn on g2 was unprotected and White's last move saw him place a bishop on a square where it too had no cover. Black takes immediate advantage by forking the two bits in question.

2 ♗xf6 ♛xg2! (Black nicks a pawn before recapturing the bishop.) **3 ♖f1** (3 ♖g1 drops the exchange to 3...♛xg1+! 4 ♘xg1 ♗xd1.) **3...gxf6 4 ♛b3 ♗xe2 5 ♗xe2 0-0-0 6 0-0-0 ♛xh2** (Black is two pawns up and comfortably goes on to convert this advantage to a full point.) **7 ♔b1 ♛f4 8 ♛c2 h5 9 ♖h1 h4 10 ♗f1 f5 11 ♗h3 ♗e7 12 ♖de1 ♗f6 13 ♖e3 ♖d7 14 ♖he1 ♖hd8 15 a3 ♔b8 16 ♔a1 c5 17 dxc5 ♛c4 18 ♖3e2 ♛xc5 19 ♛b3 ♛d5 20 ♛b4 ♛f3 21 ♖e3 ♛xf2 22 ♖3e2 ♛b6 23 ♛f4+ ♛c7 0-1**

5pts for **B**.

All of the suggested moves look quite reasonable but one stands head and shoulders above the rest:

Lugovoi – Balashov
Russia 2003

1 ♘xf6+! ♕xf6 (After 1...gxf6 2 ♗h6 ♖e8 3 ♘e5! Black's king is hopelessly exposed.) **2 ♗g5 ♗xf3**

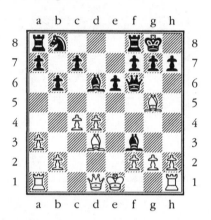

3 ♕d2! The key move. Now if you had been paying close attention to this book you would have spotted exactly the same theme earlier on. The black queen is lost and Black resigned as after **3...♗xg2** (After 3...♕xd4 White's only check is a strong one i.e. 4 ♗xh7+.) **4 ♗xf6,** for what it's worth, the capture ♗xh1 isn't possible in view of **5 ♕g5 g6 6 ♕h6.**

To round this book off then it's 5pts for **C**.

Marking Overview - Quick reference

Test One

1 D
2 B
3 E (A2pts)
4 B
5 B (A2pts)
6 D
7 C (E2pts)
8 E (A1pt)
9 D
10 C
11 B
12 C
13 C
14 D (C2pts)
15 D
16 A
17 C (E1pt)
18 E
19 A
20 A

Test Two

1 B
2 C (E2pts)
3 E
4 D
5 C
6 A
7 B
8 E
9 D
10 D
11 B
12 D (B2pts+E2pts)
13 C
14 D
15 A (E2pts)
16 B
17 E
18 C
19 D (B1pt+C1pt)
20 D

Test Three

1 E
2 B (A2pts)
3 C
4 E
5 D
6 D
7 B (A1pt)
8 A
9 D
10 C (B2pts)
11 A (B2pts)
12 C
13 D
14 B
15 A
16 C (E2pts)
17 D (B1pt)
18 C
19 E
20 E

Test Four

1	E	10	E
2	B	11	B (A1pt)
3	A (3pts)	12	C
4	A	13	E
5	C	14	D
6	C (A1pt)	15	D
7	B (D2pts)	16	A
8	D	17	E (D1pt)
9	E (C2pts)	18	D
		19	B
		20	C

Marking Scorechart

0-20
I've heard that 'snap' is quite a good game. Perhaps you might like to reconsider where your true talent lies!

21-40
Once you factor in the generous extra points I awarded, frankly you didn't do much better than the average guesser! Still at least you were game for a laugh and hopefully you should have picked up a few tips.

41-60
Now we're talking! Some of the puzzles were pretty tough and so you must be a club strength player.

61-80
You are at least of county standard and closer to the 80 mark I would suggest that you are right to harbour IM or GM aspirations.

81-90
You have performed extremely well unless you are already a Grandmaster in which case you have had an off day!

91-100
Excellent! Even Garry Kasparov might not have got 100% (depending on which test he was doing!) whilst Fritz wouldn't have scored perfectly either. If in this bracket you are right to feel proud of yourself.